TOUCHING
THE EDGE OF
Heaven

True Story of a Near-Death Experience

SARAH O'MALLEY

WESTBOW®
PRESS
A DIVISION OF THOMAS NELSON
& ZONDERVAN

Quoted from the New King James version of the
Spirit Filled Bible
New Spirit-Filled Life Bible
Copyright 2002 by Thomas Nelson, Inc.

The Holy Bible, New King James Version
Copyright 1982 by Thomas Nelson, Inc.

WestBow Press books may be ordered through booksellers or by contacting:

WestBow Press
A Division of Thomas Nelson & Zondervan
1663 Liberty Drive
Bloomington, IN 47403
www.westbowpress.com
1 (866) 928-1240

ISBN: 978-1-4908-5923-1 (sc)
ISBN: 978-1-4908-5924-8 (hc)
ISBN: 978-1-4908-5922-4 (e)

Library of Congress Control Number: 2014919913

Printed in the United States of America.

WestBow Press rev. date: 11/25/2014

CONTENTS

DEDICATION

I would like to first dedicate this book to my daddy, my papa, my best friend, the lover of my soul, the one who will never leave or forsake me, and the creator of the universe, God our Father, and His Son, Jesus Christ. I would also like to thank the Holy Spirit, who has been my counselor, teacher, and guide, giving me the strength and courage to put my heart on my sleeve in order to write this book.

I would also like to dedicate this book to my husband, my mom, my dad, my daughter, my grandchildren, and all of my family that I love very much!

FIRST FOREWORD

To watch a beauty for ashes in progress is undiscernible to the naked eye. Learning and following the hope of fulfilled dreams and goals becomes a sparkling reality.

The story in this book, I can attest, is true. I watched the transformation of a bottomed-out alcoholic, sponsoring her through the tears and the stretching of the cocoon to the fluttering of the newborn wings of faith through grace. From my perspective, I will share.

I heard the story from Sarah at a low point in her early sobriety while taking the proverbial grain of salt. Soon afterwards, in a Bible study group, I listened to a woman mention how she and her husband came upon the scene of a serious accident a couple years before. They had laid hands on this lifeless woman's body and prayed until the ambulance arrived. The hair raised on the back of my neck as I realized this woman's story matched—detail for detail—my new friend's story. They could not have known we would meet.

Experiencing this first has opened my eyes to coming to terms with this blessed gift. The joy from my friend's experience has permeated my life through the love of Jesus Christ. Because of her testimony, I came to the Lord. Watching truth of an otherwise unbelievable story became plausible in my life. I came, I came to, I came to believe. "Anything is possible if a person believes" (Mark 9:23). I now believe.

Merideth Berthiaume, Artist

SECOND FOREWORD

It is rare that we can have a true experience seen as to the awesome nature and power of our Lord. It thrills me to read this book, as it shares the truth of our miraculous, loving, omnipresent God. Sarah had two paths she could have traveled down—one with grief and pain, lost in a world of drugs and alcohol, or she could choose the path less traveled, God.

There are those who think God is the easier path, but as you will find, that is not necessarily the truth, for first God must help us see our frailty and then help us overcome that frailty. Sarah brings us through her step-by-step process, so often thinking she has reached her destination, only to find she is only in the beginning of yet a new overcoming.

Watching Sarah maturing into a woman of God and becoming ever more dependent upon the strength of God with each new overcoming was to me the very thrill of the book. It was like riding a roller coaster, the thrill of the climb upward to the mountain top mixed with the anticipation of the descent back to the valley. Each time she was led back to the valley, she was brought to a new measure of her growth to maturity.

Listen and see, if you will, "To those who can hear, let them hear," for in this book is spoken the truth of who we are and where we can be if we choose the path less traveled by. Though it looks oh so hard in the beginning, the joy received at the end is the prize we all seek.

With prayer, I hope that all who read this book are led to a new place in the Lord, as Sarah has portrayed, for God is standing at the door, waiting for the knock.

Thank you, Sarah, for standing naked for all to see who we are and that God loves us regardless.

Kathy Sarver

ACKNOWLEDGMENTS

I would like to acknowledge all the wonderful people who helped me with my first book:

To my awesome husband, Mike, who has put up with the long hours of me writing and rewriting this book, waiting patiently the whole time, while being kind, loving, and supportive—you showed me what true love is between a man and woman. I will always love you, and I am blessed with the love you give back to me.

I would like to also acknowledge my mom and dad; my daughter, my brother, my sister, my Meme, Aunty Noreen, and the rest of my family.

To my best friend, Naomi, for taking time to edit my book in the beginning and for the years and time we have spent together through my recovery—thank you for bringing me into my Holy Spirit–filled life, never asking anything in return. God has blessed me with an inspirational woman of God, and that's you. We will be bound by God's love forever!

To Kathy, for taking precious time during the holidays to edit and help convey the message clearly while looking in from the outside—you are a beautiful, prophetic woman of God whom I love dearly, and I am very blessed to have you in my life.

I would like to thank all the people who took part in my walk with God, who molded me into the woman of God that I am today: the teachers, pastors, and prophets whom God has put in my life to enlighten me, teach me, and keep me on the right path toward the prize.

CHAPTER 1

Innocence Lost

Thanksgiving Day was a bittersweet moment in time. It is a day to give thanks and praise to God for the things we share together, a day set aside with the festive mood of food, family, and friends. On this day, November 22, 1962, there came the most inconvenient birth for some on such a day as this. My mother had a son, a daughter, and then seven years later, she gave birth to an unplanned child. This child was me.

All over the country, while the aroma of turkey fills their homes, families wait patiently to take the first bite of the carefully prepared dinner. As Dr. Cohen was just about to sit down with his family for this Thanksgiving feast, he could almost taste the apple pie freshly baked for dessert. He received the call to come to the hospital to deliver me. Dr. Cohen was a family friend and delivered all three of us children.

At 5:15 p.m., I was born. It was the last place anyone would like to be on this day. As I grew up, my mom would kid around, saying, "I had my son, my daughter, and seven years later—oops, there came Sarah." She would say this every now and again, but I know now that God doesn't make mistakes. I am a precious gift to Him.

My father was a generous, kind, funny, and loving man. He had to quit junior high school to work with his father and uncle to build the family business. He would work sixty to eighty hours a week so we could live comfortably and provided for all our needs. He came home dirty and tired from doing auto mechanic work.

We lived in an upscale neighborhood with ranch, brick, and Tudor style homes. You couldn't find a yard that wasn't perfectly landscaped and manicured. We had a beautiful flowering cherry tree in the front yard; I always enjoyed the smell of the blooming pink flowers in the summer. The street we lived on was occupied with wealthy businessmen, lawyers, and doctors. We were very blessed to be able to attend the best schools and have nice clothes, and we lacked for nothing.

My mother was very beautiful. She was about five foot three with a perfect shape. She looked like a movie star, and my dad was tall, built well, and very handsome. I always loved their wedding picture hanging in their bedroom—my dad in his army uniform and my mom with her light brown hair and beautiful smile in her wedding dress. In this picture, you could see the love they had for each other. They always were dressed nice, whether they were at a summer picnic or going to a formal; you would never see them in jeans.

My sister was very shy and quiet, and when she was little, she had red curly hair and looked like a porcelain doll in all of her pictures. My brother had strawberry blonde hair, and I was born with blonde hair. We all had light skin and freckles.

My aunty Noreen was like a second mother to me. She was married to my uncle Jim, and they didn't have any children. When I was a little baby, my mom kept me in my baby carrier on the counter in the kitchen, and my aunt Noreen and uncle Jim took me for weeks at a time. Aunty Noreen told me that at one point, I even used to call them Mom and Dad. Later on in life, after they had my cousins, Aunty Noreen would load up the back of the station wagon with beach supplies and food and stuff us all in the back seat, and we would go off to the beach for the day. She would also take all of us kids in the station wagon with treats and lawn chairs to the drive-ins. Back then, they only charged by the car full, and we definitely got our money's worth. She was always taking us places and spent a lot of time with us kids!

Then there was my Meme, my father's mother. She was one of the most wonderful, loving, craziest, funniest people I ever had in my life. *Meme* means "grandmother" in French, and I adored her. She was like my mother, friend, confidant, doctor, stay-up-late movie-watching junk food partner, and most of all, the person I loved the most in the whole wide world. When my siblings, cousins, and I were all growing up, we all fought to see who would get to stay at Meme's apartment overnight on the weekends

Meme would take two or three of us at a time. She was a short French Canadian woman with deep brown eyes, puffy gray hair, and a great big smile. When I snuggled with her at night, I always pushed her hair down, and it bounced back up from all the hair spray. She used Lady Finnelle bath stuff and always smelled good. Even to this day, when I get even a small glimpse of the aroma, I think of her. She was only ticklish on her neck, so I always blew raspberries on her neck to tickle her and make her laugh.

Meme knew her Bible inside out and knew Jesus intimately. When Jesus spoke to the little children, they gathered at His feet and listened. When Meme spoke to us and told us Bible stories, we carefully listened to her calming voice. She would tell us about the beginning of creation, Adam and Eve, Noah and the ark, the Tower of Babel, and teach us about the book of Revelation and how the world was going to end. She spoke to us about the flooding, storms, and fires that would take place in the land. She told us how the animals would go extinct, and when we started to see them dead on the sides of the road, it meant we would be near the end times. You get the picture; all you have to do now is turn on the news.

My favorite times with her were when I spent those precious nights with just her and me. She was used to having different cousins there and would get my attention by calling out different names like "Paulette," "Diane," "Patricia," and "Marie." Then she'd say something like, "Okay, you little snook, get over here!"

I'd say, "Not till you say the right name, Meme!"

Then she'd say, "Anne, Jean, aha, Sarah."

That's when I would finally say, "What, Meme; are you calling me?" She loved it. She never got mad; she was always full of love, joy, patience, kindness, longsuffering, and sometimes concern when we needed to talk.

Whenever I got sick, I asked my mom or dad to bring me over Meme's house. She would make me Meme soup and give me ginger ale and hot tea. I would lie on the couch, and she would bring cold cloths and put them on my head to bring the fever down. She just loved on me. One of those times, I had a fever. While I lay on her couch, the old aunts came over to play cards. They laughed and spoke in French (so I wouldn't know what they were saying) until the later hours of the night. Then the little old lady downstairs banged her broom on her ceiling; this meant it was time for everyone to go home. It is a great memory.

Meme and I played board games like Pokeno and Yahtzee for hours at a time. We always stayed up late, ate junk food, and watched TV shows. The times we spent in that little apartment will be forever in my heart. Everyone loved Meme and wanted to be around her; even my friends from school would call her Meme.

When I started first grade, my hair was strawberry blonde. I am told I was a very happy child. I went to St. Mary's school from first to fifth grade. My Mother said this was so that I wouldn't have to come home for lunch and she could go golfing with her friends; the public schools at that time sent kids home.

At a young age, I was always the class clown and quite the talker. One day in class, I was asked by one of the nuns about my brother and sister, and I told the nuns that my siblings were Jewish and went to Jewish school. Right away, my mother was called into the school, and she explained to the head nun how she converted to Catholicism when she married my father. It's funny how kids think.

One time, my mom was on lunch duty, and I had no idea. I was talking in class to my friend Lucy and got in trouble. I ended up in Sister Superior's office, and my mom was called in. It was not a good situation for me. I was in big trouble with the nuns and when I got home.

I began taking classical piano lessons when I was seven years old. I was taught by Mrs. Miller, who lived up the street. Every day after school, I had to do my homework and practice my piano. I became very accomplished on the piano by the age of eleven. My brother was going to be in a high school talent show with his band and asked the head of the music department who was in charge of the talent show if I could play "Fur Elise" by Beethoven. They said no; I was too young, and this was for seniors. He said, "Then we're not playing!" At this time, his band was very popular among the students. So they let me play. I was a little nervous about making a mistake, but I did well. At eleven years old, I received my first standing ovation.

During the summer when I was about eight years old, my family went to Lakeside Camp, a family campground set on a farm. The entire campground went miles down to a lake where you could swim. We would all wear old pairs of sneakers when we went in because the bottom of the lake was very mucky. Our parents and all their close friends circled their trailers in the shape of a horseshoe about forty feet away from a huge fire pit. This was a great experience because it gave me two very different environments to learn and grow from. One was a small town with all its perfect little imperfections where you needed to be prim and proper, and the other was a laid-back campground on a simple farm that was only ten minutes from the most beautiful beaches you could imagine.

Our mothers stayed with us all summer long, and our fathers visited on the weekends. We would go to Ocean Beach with our older siblings during the day or to East Side Beach with our moms. Going to the beach always had such a calming effect on me, as wave after wave sang on the shore. We would body surf when the waves were really high, especially after the storms, or walk to the end of the road to get a treat at a small store by the bay down the dirt road from the jetty. We also played the old-fashioned pinball machine.

One summer, my best friend and I would walk the beach to the jetty and run to the end and back every day. The jetty was a mile long, and we knew every massive rock, crook, and cranny by heart. Sometimes we would stop and watch the fishermen set their lobster pots out in the morning on our way out to the end of the jetty, and on our way back, sometimes we would see them pulling up the lobster pots—and oh, the lobsters they would catch.

Sometimes a bunch of us kids from the campground went to the first curve of the jetty on the bay side when the tide was down. There we would jump off and swim to cool off. The best part was the prize at the end of the jetty—a lighthouse about thirty-five feet high with a loud foghorn at the top that used to sound when the fog would roll in. Sometimes we would just sit at the very end with the water crashing on the rocks on all three sides of us. When you're out there and all you can see is the wide open ocean, you ponder the mysteries that lie beneath. I felt the beauty of this massive creation and at the same time felt very small in comparison. I always get a warm fuzzy feeling in my heart, and I feel joy when I think back on those times.

At the beginning of the campground, there was a red boat with the sign "Lakeside Camp" on it. We played a game; whoever yelled "I see the red boat" first would get the first shower; whoever said it second would get the next one, and so on. After everyone showered, most families ate dinner, and we would ride our dirt bikes until it was dark. Near one of the fields in the campground, there were dirt bike trails that you could ride on for hours. One went to a main road that we didn't take very often, and the other went all the way to another part of the lake. This was a party spot for older kids at night.

Before we had a campfire, our parents would give us money to go to the camp store and get some candy, ice cream, or a soda. We would go there for a while and always tease Manny, the caretaker for the camp who ran the store after supper until about eight or nine o'clock.

On the weekends, the owner of the camp, Mr. Learner, would drive the hay wagon around the entire campground for hours. We could get on or off whenever we wanted to. There was a place we called Purple Rock at the entrance of what we called Teepee Field that was very cool. Here we would talk, meet other kids, and just hang out. It was simply seven huge rocks set across the entrance of a field, with one rock that was purple in color.

It's funny that when we were young, without any corruption in our hearts, the simple things in life became incredible places that were very real. In our imaginations, we took a simple field with rocks, and it became a place in our great imaginations where Indians used to live in teepees, chanting, drumming, and dancing in an earlier time. It would become our own special place.

Back home in our small town, as the family business grew, my mother and father threw wonderful parties for candidates running for various offices in order to raise money for their political parties. My parents also had parties and fundraising events for various charities.

We had a fully stocked bar, pool table, ping pong table, and nice wooden stereo unit. My mother went all out with shrimp cocktail appetizers, and fully catered meals. I always helped her set up and bring out the hors d'oeuvres. My parents were very close and loved each other very much; you could see how well they worked together and shined during these events. My mother complimented my father nicely.

Every year, my parents went to Bermuda with several other couples. While planning the trip, they would have cocktail parties, and I would play the piano for their guests. My father was a hardworking, well-liked man in the community and all over the state. Because of this status, my mother and father traveled, played golf, and were out of town frequently. They went golfing, then to dinner, and out with their friends. They were invited to all kinds of parities, events, and fundraisers that were of course good for them and for the business. They were very outgoing people and a lot of fun to be around.

When they were gone, I had different babysitters. There were a lot of times when my brother would take me pretty much anywhere with him, and all his friends used to call me Stinky. (They say that's because my feet used to sweat, and when I took my socks and shoes off, I had stinky feet!) One of his friends, Tommy, used to call me Little Pete. I loved being around my brother and his friends; I always felt safe. Then sometimes my sister would watch me. I know I used to drive her absolutely crazy.

But unfortunately, there was a man who was left to watch me. He watched me when I was little and right up through my childhood. He liked me a lot and was really nice to me. The problem was that he sexually abused me when I was a little child.

I remember being called into a room. There was a cabinet that contained some important books and a special hat with some jewels on it. I would go and open the doors to the cabinet to play with the items. Then he would say, "Don't play with those. If you want to play with those, you have to come up here first." So I would climb up next to him, and he would show me parts of his body and ask me to do things that were part of a game. After the game, I was allowed to play with the special items in the cabinet.

Parents beware; most sexual predators are either family or people close to the family. They don't look like creeps on the street who would invade your house or steal your child, though that does happen. They're just normal, everyday people who you would least suspect. They usually put themselves in a position near a child to groom them and gain their trust in order to take advantage.

Because of the abuse, I could only remember little bits and pieces—like Christmas time, opening up presents, riding my big wheel, and playing with my dog, or a few birthday parties— until I was about seven years old. I thought this was normal my whole life. I went to a recovery workshop later on in life and found out that people do remember their childhood back as far as two years old. I guess he just liked really little girls because starting at age seven or eight, I can remember all the things I had done in my life. I guess this was basically the beginning of memories for my life.

Beautiful houses with beautiful gardens, filled with beautiful people—sometimes things on the outside can look pretty good, but when you get a look at the inside, you never know what you will find. Looking back at my life, I don't know of any one family who didn't have some type of dysfunction going on. Unfortunately, people like to put on facades, and they suffer needlessly when they push everything under the carpet. These people walk around the elephant in the middle of the room instead of facing issues head-on.

We all have cycles from past generations that keep showing up in our everyday lives. Some are from so many decades ago that we're not even aware they exist. The only way we can change these patterns is to first acknowledge them, talk about them, and seek professional help. It doesn't matter if you're rich or poor, short or tall, or what nationality you are; these old family curses just keep popping up everywhere, and no one is excluded.

These days, doctors seem to have many names for all these concerns. I believe that God can heal and change any situation as long as all the parties involved are concerned and willing to deal with it honestly.

CHAPTER 2

Childhood Dreams Crushed

In the late sixties, I used to love hanging out with my brother; I always thought he was really cool. He had long strawberry blond hair all the way down his back and bell bottom jeans. Once he was walking down the street and surprised the guy driving by, who beeped at him, thinking he was a girl from behind because of his long hair. My brother turned around, and the guy saw his beard. I can just imagine the embarrassment on his face; it had to be priceless! This was back in the hippie days in the early '70s. My brother was always in rock-and-roll bands, and I loved listening to him play. He would take me anywhere with him, like band practices, fast car rides, sledding in the winter, and hanging out with his friends.

He took me to Gumball amusement park and talked me into going on the biggest roller coaster. I said, "I'm scared!"

He would say, "You're gonna love it. After it's over, you're going to want to go again!"

I went on and was scared, and sure enough, at the end, I said, "I want to go on again! That was fun!"

In the winter, we would go sledding with his friends, and I would go down the same steep hills as the big kids did; it was great! He was pretty good about watching me, and I always felt safe when I was with him. I can't remember how old I was the first time he moved out, but I was so sad that I couldn't stop crying. I felt like I'd lost my best friend.

Christmas time was coming. In the mid-seventies, he moved into a huge old red farmhouse with about seven other hippies. I begged my mom to let me go and stay with him for a few days. After I annoyed her enough from asking, she finally let me go. I had the best time of my life! I was about eleven years old. I found a bottle of Boone's Farm apple wine. At the time, it seemed quite harmless, probably because it didn't have much alcohol in it. Throughout the duration of the night, I drank the whole bottle. The only thing I remembered was sleeping in the upstairs middle room with the kittens.

The next afternoon, the guys went for a motorcycle ride, and I wanted to hang out with hippie girl who was there. She was very beautiful with long blonde hair, dressed in cool faded jeans and a beautifully embroidered white hippie shirt. She lit up a cigarette. I asked if I could try a puff, and she let me. It tasted horrible, but I wanted to be like her. I asked her if I could have one, and she let me. I really felt like I was one of the gang now.

I suppose my first drink of cheap apple wine and the sexual abuse as a child began the downward spiral in my life. Junior high wasn't too bad; I just never felt like I fit in. I felt very alone. I was vulnerable and wanted to fit in with the popular crowd so badly that I used to daydream about it. Coming from Catholic school, I really didn't know any of the kids in the public school.

In seventh grade, I met my best friends, Tori and Bella. We didn't start drinking and partying until the first day of high school.

On the first day of high school, Tori and Bella and I heard that there was a really cool party before school. Everyone who was anyone was going, and it was going to be held in the back of a strip mall, by a restaurant a place we called the red carpet. This was the place! It was a big red carpet laid out on the ground with a hole cut in the middle for a bonfire.

We didn't live near there but wanted so badly to fit in with the cool kids that we had our own party. I went to my dad's well-stocked liquor cabinet and decided to take a bottle of gin and a two-liter bottle of orange soda. We met on the path that was on the way to school. We wanted to be cool like all the in-crowd kids. Needless to say, Tori, Bella, and I drank the whole thing. It tasted terrible, and I'm sure that I drank most of it.

In first period gym class, I sat on the bleachers, trying to listen to the teacher. All of a sudden, the room started spinning, and I ran into the girl's locker room to visit the old porcelain toilet. I threw everything up and only made it to a few of my last classes. Needless to say, I never drank gin again. To this day, I can't stand the smell of it; it makes me sick to my stomach.

In our family, having a party or drinking on the weekends was the norm, and my drinking and partying became more important than my school work. It was my sophomore year in high school, and I was getting Cs, Ds, and too many Fs. We would drink and party on the weekends, bringing booze and smoking pot before school dances. Skipping school to go out for breakfast was the norm, and we sometimes got high on the way back to school.

I felt numb inside, but people couldn't tell on the outside. I hated school and all the cliques in it. There were jocks, freaks, and nerds. I didn't fit in to any one of those categories, so I was the class clown and used humor to get out of myself and my feelings of numbness. I had all the things that most girls that age would want—a car, nice clothes, and money—but there was always that feeling of emptiness.

My mother and I often fought and argued. She wasn't always around to bring me up, so the school system and the world brought me up. When my mother would ground me and tell me to be home by 10:00 p.m., my parents weren't home to enforce it. Sometimes they wouldn't get home until one or two in the morning. So I decided to try to get home before they did. Sometimes I would get caught, and other times I wouldn't.

I never really cared what my mom thought, but I didn't like it if my dad was mad at me. When he got mad, he just wouldn't talk or laugh with me, and that would hurt the most. He always worked so much, and when he was around, everybody wanted to be near him. He was funny and kind. I cherish those moments with my dad.

My mother couldn't figure out what to do with me, so she went to the school principal and counselors and asked for some advice. They decided to give me an IQ test. When the test results came back, they found out that I had the second highest IQ in the entire class. The principal said that I was too smart and just very bored in my classes, never taking a second look that I might have had other issues.

I got in so much trouble my sophomore year that my mother sent me to an all-girls private school so they could fix me, and I had to stay back that year. I remember the first day like it was yesterday. We drove into this fancy girls' school. On my left, I could see girls wearing pleated skirts playing field hockey and big old houses on the campus where girls from around the world lived on campus. Rolling my eyes, all I could think was, *I have just arrived in a deep dark fiery bottomless pit.*

I was given a tour of the facility and met with the headmaster. I saw all the fake teachers with their plastic smiles. The whole time, all I thought was, *Can someone please get me out of this place?*

On my first day of school, I looked to my right and saw a girl weeping and crying as her mom told her to get out of the car and go to school. She was an acquaintance from my old high school. I said, "Holly."

She turned and looked and said, "Sarah, they're sending you here too?" She stopped crying, and we hugged and went into the school together.

As time went on, two more girls were sent there from our town. Our mother's drove us back and forth to the school, and it wasn't so bad. I studied and brought all my grades up, and I made some friends with girls from other countries and cities. I still hung out with my hometown high school friends on the weekends. I dreaded going to that school every day, so my mother said if I brought my grades up to A's and B's, I could go back to my old school. By the end of the year, all my grades were up to A's and B's, so my mother let me go back.

When I returned, all my friends were seniors, and I was just a junior. The kids in my class were all underclassmen, and all my friends were now seniors. I was miserable and felt unattached and alone. Again, I hated school and not even being in the same classes with my best friends. At least they were there, and we could do things after school. I kept my grades up so I could stay there. In the year 1980, my friends all graduated.

When I got my license, I would drive over to my Meme's house and visit her a few times a week. Once a week, we went out to her favorite place for dinner called the Eatery. It was mostly for older people, didn't cost too much, and didn't have too many spices, so it was easy on her stomach. I would pull up in my car, and there she waited, looking out the window for me. As soon as I walked up the stairs, I gave her a huge hug and kiss, blew raspberries on her neck, made her say, "you little snook," and both of us would laugh! She was great to be around and very full of life.

There was a really special dinner once a year on her birthday. I always dressed up and brought her a dozen long-stem yellow roses. She loved yellow roses and said, "I like these the best because yellow means forever." Anytime I see long-stem yellow roses, I can see her smile in my mind and a warm feeling of love comes over me and fills my heart with joy.

That summer was great! I had a car, went to graduation parties, went to the beach when I wanted, and was able to hang out at pool parties in town. I basically had the freedom to do what I wanted.

I had a job at the pizza place in town and lots of friends. I just moved with the world, checking out different bands and parties and taking weekend trips with my friends. Partying became more prominent in my life.

Then the school year began. I was in the class of 1981. I had never felt more alone. All my friends were working or going off to college or another country. In every class, there were classmates I didn't even know, and everywhere I looked, there was no one. Every day, I dreaded going to school even more than I ever did before. I had all A's and B's because I had no friends.

I couldn't believe what my life had become. I was in a world of darkness with small-town, stiff-necked people and nowhere to hide. Because I had turned eighteen, I would write notes for myself for being late to school, and the only thing I could think of was going out to the bars on the weekends with my friends so I could drink, dance, and get out of myself. I would argue and fight with my mom, and she finally said, "If school is making you that miserable, then quit. Just get your GED so you can at least get a job or go to a community college." So I quit school, got my GED, and just worked at the pizza place.

One night, I was out with my friends in a bar. I had been drinking and minding my own business with my girlfriend. We were on our way out, and guy pinched my butt. With the mixture of self-defense, alcohol, years of angry emotions running frantically through my heart, and music blaring from the jukebox, I turned and said to him, "Oh, you don't know who you're messing with." I knocked him down and started kicking him in the leg until someone pulled me off of him.

My friends pulled me out of the bar and brought me home. I thought I showed him what he deserved for his inappropriate behavior. He was taken to the hospital and received many stiches in his leg. He never pressed any charges against me; I think he was embarrassed because he did not defend himself from a girl.

I'd become numb to all humanity. I blamed him for touching me and justified this reaction in my head; it was unreal. In karate class, we were taught that if you want to kill someone, you're in the wrong place and should go buy a gun, as karate is for self-defense. But if anyone goes past the line—touches you inappropriately or hits you first—all bets are off. After this incident, I dropped out of karate; I decided not to fight anymore. It's a shame I didn't realize the root of the problem and quit drinking too.

The summer of 1981, my best friend, Bella, and I headed off to the beach. All I did was party all night and lie on the beach all day. I got a job waitressing in one of the hottest nightclubs around at the age of eighteen. My drinking on the weekends became more advanced, and I learned the great art of staying awake all night by using cocaine. I did so much coke that summer that halfway through the season, I didn't want to use it anymore. I saw things I had never seen before.

The latest and best up-and-coming rock and roll bands were featured at the club I worked at. I met and partied with famous people. One afternoon, my parents came down, and my mother demanded that I come home. I told them to go away; there was nothing they could do. I can still remember the sadness in my father's face before they walked away. I felt bad for him, but I was eighteen, and I was going to do what I wanted.

It was at the end of the season, and the fall was quickly approaching; the fun, crazy summer at the beach was coming to an end. The owner of the bars threw a huge end-of-the-season party for us, and a few days after, I received a phone call from my father. He said, "I got a job for you at the Courthouse, and you start tomorrow. Come home." I decided to go home; after all, where else was I going to go? One day, I was lying on the beach, and the next, I was dressed up working in the Courthouse.

Talk about a culture shock. But because I was a person who could change and reinvent herself in any environment, I was ready for a new adventure. I started working a high-paying job with

17

benefits; I was somebody. This was the job that anyone would be grateful for, but of course I wasn't. My heart had become so cold and I was so bitter over what my life had become that I just didn't care—I couldn't. I took everything for granted.

I made a couple of new friends to go out to lunch with, and on Fridays, we would go to happy hour next door. The owner of this establishment would bring everyone free drink chips on Fridays. The older women would give us all of their chips, and we would go out on Friday after work and tie a good one on.

When I was nineteen, my Meme became very sick. She was a very religious Catholic woman of God who read her Bible and prayed the rosary continuously, probably praying for all of us crazy kids. The difference between her and the rest of the world was that she had a relationship with God and was very in tune with the Holy Spirit.

Meme had many gifts of discernment; she was a seer and a prophet. There were times when I would walk into her house and pretend to be happy but had big problems on my mind. I couldn't get anything past her. She would say, "What's wrong?"

I'd say, "Nothing, Meme. Let's go out to dinner."

She would gently say, "Come over here and sit. Tell me what's wrong." Then we would talk it out before we went to dinner. She would always say, "You can't enjoy a good dinner if you have too much stuff on your mind." She was right.

As time went by, she found out that she had throat cancer. This came from smoking too many cigarettes in her earlier days. She had to have surgery to remove the cancer. The night before her surgery, she made me promise her that if anything were to happen to her, I would make sure that Janet didn't come to her funeral. I said, "Meme, nothing is going to happen to you." She took my hand and made me look into her eyes and promise on God's Word that if anything would happen to her, I would make sure that Janet did not attend her funeral.

18

Janet was the woman who married my Pepe after he divorced my Meme. Meme wasn't the only one who disliked Janet, but that's a whole different book. So I promised on God's Holy Bible that I would not ever let this happen. She had her surgery, and after she recovered, she went to Worcester to a healing service. She received prayer and a healing cloth that she would hold on her neck as she prayed. She was healed; her Lord and Savior, Jesus Christ, healed her.

After about a year and a half, Meme had to have another surgery due to a tumor or cancer of some kind. This time, she did not recover. She was in the hospital for a long time. I worked for my Aunty Noreen at a convenience store at the time. I would go to work, go to the hospital, have a few drinks, and go home to bed. This routine continued for about a year or so. It was very hard to see her in such pain, day after day. We wouldn't leave her alone in the hospital, so one of the family members was there most of the time.

Meme was finally moved to her own apartment on a hospital bed in her living room. The nurses would come by once a day, and we all took different shifts to take care of her. My Aunty Noreen used to give her all of her shots, and one day, she just couldn't do it, so I had to. This was one of the hardest things I ever had to do. There was my Meme, seventy-six years old and in a hospital bed in her living room. At the age of nineteen, I couldn't even imagine that someday, this would be me.

This incredible woman of God was shrinking to almost nothing, lying there quietly, helpless. The woman who taught me how to live would teach me how to die. She reached the point where she couldn't eat or drink anything and just had a tube in her. She pulled the tube out when she wanted to be at peace. She hung on for three days with nothing in her; it was like she was waiting for something.

Then the time came. On April 1, 1982, we were all around her, and the bishop she had been waiting for came to see here. He came and greeted us and had a little sermon for my Meme. He blessed our family, and then he left. She lifted her head up, which would be impossible at this point without food or water. She looked at each and every one of us with a huge smile on her face. She looked up at the ceiling, and it was like she saw Jesus. Her face was smiling and bright. Then a ray seemed to come from heaven, and her soul was lifted up to God. It was done.

My father planned her funeral, and everyone made arrangements. The night before her wake, I had a dream in which my Meme was at the end of my bed, reminding me of the promise I made to her. She said in a soft voice, "Remember, do not let her come to my wake or my funeral." And as soon as I was going to reply, she was gone. That morning, in a panicked state, I called my dad and said, "You can't let Janet come the wake or the funeral."

Dad said, "She's not going to come."

I said, "Call Pepe and find out. I promised Meme she wouldn't be there." I told him that if I had to stand outside the whole time, I would; I wasn't going to let her in. So to relieve my mind, my father called my Pepe. We found out she was actually planning to attend. Did this woman not have any respect? My dad told her not to come because he wouldn't let her in anyway. I was glad he had called. Thankfully, she did not come.

The day before the funeral, I made arrangements to pick up enough long-stemmed yellow roses for all of my cousins and me to put down on her grave after the service. It was our own special way of saying a little prayer, saying good-bye, and honoring her for the last time on earth. Yellow means forever to me now more than ever. Someday, I'll walk with her again in heaven. I miss her very much.

I became pregnant at the age of twenty. I was only a size one, eighty-five pounds, and five foot three. I missed my period after the third month. I went to Dr. Cohen, the doctor who delivered me, and found out I was pregnant. During our usual visits, he would always joke around with me and say, "You're the little one who ruined my turkey dinner." This time he wasn't so happy, because he knew my parents, and I was not married.

I was four months along, and when I heard my baby's heartbeat for the very first time, I quit drinking, smoking, and doing drugs for the rest of my pregnancy. I was afraid to tell Dr. Cohen about the drinking and drugs I had done. I was carrying a new life inside my body—my very own child. I had to make sure the baby would be healthy.

When my parents first found out I was single and pregnant, they were very upset. I don't believe my dad said a word for at least three days. My mom told me to go in my room or get out of the house when she had friends over; she was embarrassed and didn't want anyone to know the disgrace I had brought to the family. After a few months went by, they moved me to a condo in a small town near my brother's house so he could keep an eye on me. I was about six months along in my pregnancy. It was a nice, two-bedroom townhouse in a good neighborhood. The complex had a large pool, baby pool, and swings. It was the perfect place to have a baby.

On June 16, 1985, I had a beautiful baby girl. I named her Laura. When the doctors put her in my arms, I felt a love for her like I never had known before. She had a head full of dark brown hair, brown eyes, and beautiful skin. I held this little life that depended on me in my arms. I looked into my precious daughter's eyes for the first time, not knowing how to be a mother. I was afraid, nervous, and exited all at the same time. She was incredibly beautiful. I had so many emotions running through me that they brought tears to my eyes.

I became pregnant after my Meme died, and I believed that my daughter was a present from God. I wanted to do everything right. I started by breastfeeding her because I heard that it was the healthiest thing for her. When it was time to feed her baby food, I cooked fresh vegetables and crushed them up to go along with her oatmeal. I was ecstatic; it was one of the happiest times in my life during which I was most content.

I had a baby pack that I would put her in, and we would go everywhere together—shopping, on walks, to the pool, and to visit people. I loved on my daughter every minute of the day and night. I was a new mom, and she became my new life.

I grew up living a very sheltered life in a small town, always hanging around with people I grew up with. I was all by myself in a different setting with my new baby, in the world all alone, and doing the best I could. My life was about to change drastically and take a turn for the worse. I was still breastfeeding my daughter, and she was about three months old. I kept to myself and didn't bother with anyone.

There were men painting the condominium complex I lived in. One of the painters was a friend of a friend's brother. This friend was a girl I knew in the complex who I used to walk with a couple times a week. On the really hot days when they would work on my part of the condos, I would make ice tea for them.

One night at about eleven thirty, Laura was sleeping in her crib, and I heard a knock at the door. I asked who was there, and a man replied, "It's me." He was one of the guys painting the complex. "I need to come in and use your phone. I'm having trouble with my car and don't know what else to do."

I said through the door, "Maybe you should ask someone else. It's really late, and my baby's sleeping."

Then he said, "Please, I just got in a big fight with my girlfriend. I'm so upset, and now my car won't start. Can you please let me in, just for a minute to use the phone? I won't be long."

Feeling sorry for him, I opened the door. He came in the house, locked the door behind him, and said, "Don't say a word; just kiss me."

I answered, "No way; I don't want to kiss you."

He said, "Kiss me right now." He tried to kiss me, and I pushed him away. I tried to pull away from him, but he began to hit me and said, "If you scream, I will kill your baby." He then pulled me upstairs to my bedroom and raped me for hours. Laura woke up in the middle of this. He let me feed her and put her back in her crib. He continued raping me for what seemed like an eternity, and then he left.

I tried to shower away the incident, but in the end, I just sat and stared in a daze. I felt empty, dull, weak, numb, and afraid. It was like someone took away all the joy, love, peace, and freedom of raising my daughter right out of me. I felt ashamed and disgusted with life. A huge part of me was ripped out and crushed. As fear overwhelmed me, the only way I could go on was to block it out of my mind and act like it never really happened at all.

For many years, I continued to have nightmares about the rape. As I woke up from a dream of him beating me, I could hear him saying, "If you make a sound, I'll kill your baby." I dreamed of being tied to the bedpost and crying softly to myself as he continued to rape me. I would wake up in a cold sweat with chills and my heart pounding out of my chest, just like it happened yesterday. After these dreams, I'd shake and clench my blanket, hanging on for dear life. I would look around, and it would take a few minutes to realize that I was home in my own bed, and I was going to be all right..

Laura was the sunshine in my life that kept me going. I had something to live for, someone to love and take care of. I believe that she is the reason I could move on. I just blocked it from my mind and life like it never happened. I poured my life into my beautiful daughter and moved on. They say perfect love casts out all fear, and she was the love of my life.

When a woman gets raped, she either goes to the police or blocks it out of her memory like it never happened. I blocked it out, but the nightmares still kept coming. It was my nasty little secret that made me feel dirty, ashamed, and not good enough. I went on living my life as usual, like nothing happened. I was terrified that if I told anyone, he would come back and possibly do something worse.

Laura turned nine months old, my best friend, Tori, got married. This was the first time I had gone out since I had Laura. My mom came and babysat, and I went to the wedding, came back to check on her, and then went to the reception. At the wedding, I ran into a friend who was a drummer. He said his band was playing every other month near where I lived, and I should come check it out sometime. I kept that in the back of my mind.

When Laura was about eleven months old, I started working at a local pub, and a fifteen-year-old girl I met in the complex earlier that year babysat for me while I worked. I had been clean and sober since I found out I was pregnant with Laura. This was a great little town pub where everyone knew everyone. There were different musicians coming in and out, playing acoustic music that I enjoyed very much. I loved working and hearing good music at the same time, and the tips were really good, too. I also liked having my days free to spend with Laura.

I heard that my friend's band was playing on a night I wasn't working, and I decided to go out. The band was good, and I had a soda. Then I had my first drink and a cigarette. I stayed for a few sets, talked to my friend in between, and then went home. A few weeks later, I had another drink after work, and it slowly started the progression of drinking again.

One night, a tall man with long hair walked in and told me I was going to be his wife. I found this to be amusing. He was a musician, and we began to play music together. I let him into my life. He asked me to marry him, and I said yes. After all, I was in love. I found out later, I was in love with the idea of being in love and the happily ever after. I had no clue what real love was.

I thought he was like a knight in shining armor and would always protect us. He told me he loved me, and I was mesmerized by his musical talent and how much attention he gave me. He was in a band, and I liked to go out and see it once in a while. I let him move in with me after two months, and being pretty much atheist at this point in my life, I didn't have any convictions this was not the right thing to do.

As a young girl, I always dreamed of getting married and having a big wedding outside, so we planned a huge wedding outside. I told my dad as he drove me there that I felt like Cinderella going to the ball. We had a beautiful ceremony. We found a minister, who really didn't have any good advice about getting married or what that would entail, and it didn't matter what faith we were; he just married us. At this time, we were partying together on the weekends. I had a few drinks before I was married, and we both had a few shots before we walked into the reception. It was just one big party with an open bar and large buffet

Laura was almost two years old when we were married. For our honeymoon, we went to the Bahama's. It was full of gorgeous beaches, beautiful people, and fabulous dining. We came home and played music together, and he became so jealous of any other man's attention that he split my lip open after three weeks of being married. He said he was sorry, that he didn't know what came over him, and that he would never do it again, so I forgave him and stayed.

He decided to move Laura and me far away from my friends and family. I had no idea that the abuse would continue or even get worse. I was only in my early twenties and lacked the wisdom that I have now. It's clear to me today that abusers tend to move you away from loved ones to have control and power to abuse you and make you more vulnerable and afraid to leave. At the time, I was smitten with him and didn't want to believe something like that would happen again.

One night, after putting Laura down for the night, we had a fight, and he started choking me. I couldn't breathe, and I thought he was going to kill me. I felt like I was going to die. Right when I thought I had no oxygen left, he stopped. He began apologizing like he always did. He would say, "I'm so sorry, I love you, and I'll never do it again." As I pulled away, I scrunched up in the corner of the room, shaking. He tried to touch me and say he was sorry.

I just shook as I curled up in the fetal position, crying out, "Leave me alone." This was not the first or second time—as a matter of fact, I couldn't count any more. Who was this man? I knew this was not how a marriage was supposed to be. Concerned for my daughter and my safety, I finally left him. The marriage lasted about three months.

CHAPTER 3

Downcast Is My Soul

With my tail between my legs and Laura being a little over two years old, I ended up moving back home with my parents. It was really hard for my parents and for my daughter and me. I was used to being on my own. There was no privacy at my parents' house. I also felt like we were intruding on their personal space.

My parents left for Texas for the winter, so I had to find a sitter while I worked at night. I was still blocking out the incident of my childhood when I agreed to allow a young man, a relative, to babysit for Laura. He was in high school still and needed extra money, and my mom thought it would be okay, so I had him babysit for Laura.

I later found out that he sexually abused her, and I wanted to kill him. I couldn't believe that someone in my family would abuse a small child like this. I was still blocking out the horrid memory from my past. I was horrified and wanted to lock him up in jail forever and throw away the key. I felt guilt, shame, and disgust. How could I let this happen? How could I not have known—my baby, my beautiful baby girl? I wanted to kill him, and then people told me that if I killed him, I'd end up in jail, and who would protect Laura from other people? What would happen to her?

My family members pleaded with me and talked me into letting him get professional help for the family's sake. Though I wanted to see him in jail for what he did, I let my family talk me into sweeping the incident under the carpet so no one would be embarrassed, he could get professional help, and I could tend to my daughter's needs. I still wonder to this day if I did the right thing. He should have paid the consequences for his actions. I was very bitter and angry—angry at myself for letting it go, and angry at my family for once again sweeping it under the carpet.

Finally, I landed a decent job with good pay and benefits. We moved into a small two-bedroom house in another small town. Laura started going to school, and I worked during the day. But deep down inside, I was always searching for something more. I was at a very vulnerable point in my life and started dabbling in the occult.

I joined a coven of witches who were supposedly white witches. They explained to me that there were white, gray, and black witches. The white witches practiced a religion in which we could celebrate holidays for Mother Earth. There would be new moon and full moon rituals during which we would chant and pray to gods that were found in ancient Greek mythology that were not even real, and because they were white witches, there was no real harm in it. I felt like I finally belonged somewhere, to something.

We met once a week at a witch's house and learned how to make a circle and call the elements from the east, west, north, and south. We all got black robes, and then we were to be trained for a year. The year of training would teach us all of the festivals of the new moon, full moon, and harvest, and on Halloween, we had a special ritual. The veil between life and death was to be the thinnest, and we were told we could speak to people who died within the last year. After the year was over, she would evaluate us and ask us questions to see if we passed the test of becoming witches.

The first one to be asked was a man, and he passed the test. Then it was my turn, and I didn't get it. I still thought it was just an earth religion in which I could take care of Mother Earth. I now realize that it's all demonic, and they are worshiping Satan and trying to usher in the lost, vulnerable people who are broken and searching for something more. During their rituals, they use your energy to do their bidding; they tell you nothing about this. They cast spells on other people. I now know that there is no difference between white, gray, or black witches; they're all the same. They're all demonic and calling upon Satan, pretending to be nice to reel you in.

It was during this time I met a tall, handsome man. I thought he was different from all the other guys; he was clean-cut and dressed nice, unlike the man I was with before. He didn't yell at me, hit me, or not let me talk to my family or friends. He would buy me things like jewelry and take me out to dinner. He helped me redo my kitchen and treated me like a precious rose petal. After about three months of dating, he began speaking of how much he loved me and how beautiful it was to live in the woods.

We drove by a house for sale every now and again. The house had a field stone fireplace, stained glass windows, a wraparound porch, and two bedrooms. It looked like an English cottage that I had always dreamed about, like one you would find somewhere in the Welsh countryside. So he went to the bank, got the loan, and bought the cottage. It was the perfect place to live, after all, and he was the kind of man I always wanted to be with—someone who would take care of Laura and me and make all my dreams come true. I was finally going to live happily ever after.

We moved in together and went on a beautiful vacation to the mountains. It was the perfect storybook life that every girl could ever dream of having. I made some new friends, and we went out every Friday night to the local pub. There was a swimming hole right down the road, and when it was hot during the summer, we would just walk down the road and go swimming. When Laura started school, I worked part time in the mornings. Life was really good.

Slowly, little fights started, and then reality set in. We started arguing and fighting constantly. I couldn't do anything right, and he became verbally abusive. My daughter was now at an age where she knew what was going on. The more we fought, the more I would drink to get away from him. He was very jealous, and I couldn't go anywhere, talk to anyone, or look at anyone. The only place I could go to escape reality was in the bottle. Drinking brought me into my own little world.

The fights were every weekend, so every weekend, I drank. If I did something he didn't like, he would call me inappropriate names, and then it would escalate into an argument. He emotionally abused me by calling me demeaning words. The words that were spoken over me every day began to define who I was. I was walking on eggshells twenty-four-seven. If you've ever been in a similar situation, you know how hard this is to manage. This is a very unhealthy relationship for anyone. This is a vicious cycle of being in love with a man and never really knowing what true love really is.

Every Friday night, I got a sitter and went out. I would see all my friends, dance, and have a good time until he argued and fought with me. I could only dance with one of his friends so he wouldn't get mad, and he would always get mad for one reason or another. We would have to leave, and he would start a fight on the way home. I began having anxiety attacks and seeing a doctor. Most of the fights were not around my daughter—not yet, anyway.

Years passed, and Laura was in junior high school. Being the brilliant man he was, my husband said that if we moved away from this town and all the friends I had, we wouldn't fight anymore, and the anxiety would stop. I was around twenty-nine years old, and we started looking for a new home. We found a large house with a fireplace on two acres with a natural look of blooming flowers for every season besides winter. The landscaping was impeccable, the school system was excellent, and it was an even nicer dream house than the first one.

At this point, I was a mess. I was filled with anxiety from the things I had already been through in life, and I just went along with it. I had no idea of getting a job or getting out of this relationship. I was anxious, broken, and not a good mother, as I put my daughter in this situation. But he claimed this was going to save our relationship and make it all better.

I can now see the pattern; I picked bad, controlling, abusive, and unhealthy men. This is something I learned later on in life from my friend, Carlisle. She would say, "Sarah, you have a really bad picker." You keep picking out men who want to control you, and keep you away from your loved ones, friends and family

The first three weeks were wonderful, like we never had a problem at all. It was just like the beginning—and then, of course, the abuse started and escalated. At this point, he was physically abusing me. I was not a healthy person, because after six years, I still wanted to try to make this relationship work. What an embarrassment this would be to my family if I failed at yet another marriage—to the man they couldn't stand in the first place. Oh, if I had only listened to them.

We went to counseling a few times and even tried different counselors. He didn't like any of them and refused to go any more. He didn't need any help; it was always my fault. So I found a woman counselor who I saw once a week and a psychiatrist who gave me my medications to keep me from having anxiety attacks.

Life as I knew it was not worth living. He was so controlling over me that any spare time I had was spent with him and not with my daughter. She had to rely on spending time with friends or be home by herself. She always had food in the fridge, a roof over her head, and clothes on her back. I was not there for her spiritually, mentally, or emotionally. I was a terrible mother; I couldn't even take care of myself.

One morning, when Laura was at school, I decided to take a shower. I began to have a flashback of the rape. My heart began to pound, and my entire body shook. He came home for lunch and found me curled up in the shower, crying and shaking in the fetal position. He pulled me into the bedroom and gave me a few Clonazapine to stop the attack. I slept it off, and when I woke up, I felt like my life was slowly fading away from me. I had lost control of my life, and I was not a good mother. A deep, dark despair set in.

As I received help from my psychiatrist and my awesome counselor, I began to get the anxiety attacks under control and didn't have them as often, until the day came when I didn't have them anymore. My husband called me a leech because I didn't contribute to the bills or have a job, so when my daughter turned fourteen, I would take her to work with me after she came home from school.

Life with this man was so bad that I didn't want to leave her alone with him. Things escalated to the point where I knew I had to leave him. If I had a job and worked, he said I was cheating on him. If I stayed home and kept house, he said that I was a no-good leech. I always felt like I was stuck between a rock and a hard place.

We finally reached a point where I was paying all the bills, working six days a week, and getting abused by this man. He couldn't keep a job for more than a half a year and would spend all his pay on pot. I decided it was time to leave for good.

I derived a new plan. I paid off my car, packed important pictures and paperwork, and went through things, slowly waiting for the right moment to leave. I had to be very careful because he said if I ever left him, he would kill me. He said that if he couldn't have me, no one would. That's another way abusers use fear to keep you where they want you. They make you believe that they will kill you so you will be too afraid to leave or tell anyone else. So the weeks went by, and somehow he sensed that I was going to leave him.

The day came when Laura was at school. He said he knew I was leaving, so he helped me out. He dragged me out of the house by my hair and said, "You want to leave? Get out." So I got in my car and left. I went to the school to get my daughter and was on my way to my brother's house. My husband followed me in his truck, trying to say he was sorry (once again), so I pulled into the police station and started beeping my horn in a panic until two police officers came out.

I told the officer that my husband was abusive and wanted to kill me. I wanted him to leave me alone so I could go somewhere safe. The officer let me leave while he made my ex stay so he couldn't follow me. My daughter and I were finally safe at my brother's house. This was the third time I had left him. I feared for my life and never went back again.

We stayed at my brother's house for about three weeks. I felt safe there, but I felt like I was interfering in their lives. My brother hid me in a hotel for a few months. I had no idea what I was going to do. I had quit my job and was living in fear that he would find and harm us. I went to visit my very old, dear friend, Harvey. He had an apartment above the Liquor store in the town where we used to live. He said, "Come stay at my place. You and Laura should absolutely not be living in a hotel. Come and stay here until you get settled." Harvey took us in, and in turn, I cooked, cleaned, and took care of him and the apartment. He was about seventy-five years old and needed the help anyway.

Laura and I shared a room, and we stayed there for quite some time. Harvey lived near Jamestown Church. A Christian woman lived across the street named Lydia. Lydia would come over to visit and watch *Little House on the Prairie* with him. I thought she was nice for a church lady. She kept trying to get Harvey and me to go to church, but it never happened.

When I was living with my ex, I made beaded jewelry and sold it at fairs. The church lady was talking about the church bazaar and how she was looking for items to sell, so I gave her all the jewelry I made. I told her take the jewelry, sell it, and give the money to the church; I did not want to have any reminders of the ex or anything to do with that part of my life.

Harvey once spoke about the two times he actually went to Jamestown Church. He pulled out a few Bibles he had and gave me one. Harvey was one of my dearest and closest friends. This is why I am so grateful now that he signed it for me and I kept it safe all these years. He has passed since then and will forever be in my heart. The Bible he gave me will always be my favorite Bible.

CHAPTER 4

Pulled into the Depths of Darkness

After staying at Harvey's for a time, I moved to a little house in Jamestown of my own with a fieldstone fireplace. My dad built a closed-in front porch on it. It looked just like a cozy Welsh cottage. It had a cute little kitchen, and I painted the whole place. Laura and I were settled in and happy there. I had great concerns of my ex coming after me, so I had my best friend's brother come and live with us. He stayed in the spare room, and I felt safe having him there. I bought a horse named Honey who resided in my back yard. We had two dogs and a bird named Song.

My life had become one big party; the only thing I accomplished was taking care of my animals, making sure Laura did well in school, working to pay the bills, and partying. The only source of peace that I had was riding Honey every day. She was beautiful. She was a quarter horse with light auburn coloring and a brown mane and tail. We had the best relationship out of anyone I knew at the time. She would walk, trot, and canter using voice command. I could go swimming with her (which is something horses won't do unless they trust you totally). The only time I gave her a kick was when we went into a full run. That was one of the best feelings I knew at this point in my life. Honey could take me places where no one could go, like a mountain top with a valley and a lake in the middle with no one else around except for me, her, and God's creation.

I was still a weekend warrior party animal and stayed sober during the week. Every day, I baled hay, worked out in the gym, rode my horse, and bartended part-time. This was how I paid the bills. I hated almost every human being on the face of the earth, except for my daughter and my small circle of friends (or so I thought). I never thought I had a drinking problem or that my heart had become cold and turned to stone. At this point in my life, I was numb to the things around me. Family was a distant memory, and I was just moving with the world with no goals or direction. I just took life moment to moment.

As time went on, my roommate became my boyfriend. We were living in sin, but it really didn't matter to me anymore. I trusted him because I was best friends with his sister, who was my favorite drinking buddy, and I have known the both of them since Laura was about eight years old. Of course, he was perfect, funny, and probably one of the nicest men I have ever been with. He drank like I did on the weekends, and he was nice to me and Lindsay. He looked like a mountain man. He was big and burly with dark hair and a beard. His laugh would echo through the house, and life was light and fluffy.

I thought that I was smarter than him because he would do whatever I wanted him to; I think he really did love me. He never laid a hand on me; he was the perfect one for the moment. I hung around with people in bands who liked to party like I did. These were some unusual people who invited me to some pretty strange parties. I saw things that most people wouldn't see in a lifetime. Then again, this generation seems to have far surpassed anything I could have imagined.

I was running down a wide-open road with my eyes wide shut. Everything around me was filled with evil. I thought I was God. If people didn't do what I wanted, when I wanted, how I wanted, they could let the door hit them on the way out. I didn't care about anything except my daughter and my animals, and of course, Josh; he was good to me.

I was blindly moving with the wickedness in the world, drinking on the weekends until I blacked out. I was a legend in my own mind. I thought if I ever walked into a church, the walls would fall down because I was so evil. All the bad words spoken over me became my reality. My daughter was old enough to stay at a friend's house or home alone. When the bar closed down, I could go to an after party; if there was no after party, we would make one. I would go out singing with friends in bands and think I was a rock star, and all the other people were like trash to me. There was nothing left for me. I would wake up with a hangover and just hang my head and cry. I knew something was very wrong but had no idea how to fix it or cared to even try.

My mom said to me, "Sarah, you can't hate everyone all the time. Someday, you're going to grow old and be all alone." I did not care at all. Later in life, I went through some old family photo albums. There were no pictures of me at any of the family gatherings. I was too busy for family and friends who really cared about me, caught up in the relentless, wicked ways of the world. I could not see the endless black pit my life had become.

The days were dark, the nights were long, and I had no love left inside of me. People used me, and I used them; my motives were purely evil. I began riding my horse every day alone. That's the way I liked it—alone. The guy I was living with was going out with his friends all the time, and I was going out with mine. Things seemed dark and out of control, and I just existed. Discontentment and destruction took over. People I played music with couldn't deal with my perpetual attitude, and honestly, neither could I.

CHAPTER 5

Encompassed in the Light of God

It was a cold, bleak, rainy night on November 15, 2001. It started off like any normal Thursday night would. I was not able to contemplate the events that were about to unfold. I attended the Thursday night horse auction with my roommate to watch the different horses as they trotted by. I found it to be relaxing to sit and have a beer while watching horses, saddles, leads, and other equipment being auctioned off. I asked my daughter to come with me, and she declined. After the auction, we stopped for a late dinner and a few drinks and then went to another establishment for a few more drinks.

As we headed for home, a cold, sharp rain striking the windshield, we drove along Highway 202. I saw the bright headlights of a Mack truck coming up fast from behind us. It rear-ended the back of my Nissan. I heard shattering glass and screeching tires on cement. I went through the back side window, shattering the glass with my body. I soared thirty feet in the air onto cement. I landed on the V between the highway and the exit ramp. My left leg was dislocated and up behind my head. My body was cut all over from the glass and being thrown onto the pavement. There I lay, with blood and glass all over me.

All I remember is a huge flash of light. I felt like a huge bird with enormous wings picked me up by my shoulders and pulled me up, higher and higher. The loud, thundering sound of its wings seemed to shake my entire being. Every time I was pulled up another notch, I heard the thundering wings and saw a face from my past. I would look deep into their eyes, into the depths of emotion in their souls. I saw one face at a time, like on a 33mm film that hadn't been developed yet and was pulled out from the camera. As I looked deep into their eyes, I felt the emotion that I gave to that person from a moment in time.

The first face I saw was the face of a little girl I was mean to and teased when I was young a long time ago in the house I grew up in. I felt the hurt, pain, and sadness in her heart, how lost, alone, and deep in despair she felt in that moment.

Then the bird pulled me up again with the thundering sound of its wings, shaking everything. I saw another face in the film— like an old boyfriend. While I looked into his eyes, I felt the pain deep down in his heart at the moment I broke up with him. This feeling penetrated deep into my soul.

As the bird's thundering wings pulled me up, I saw yet another face on the film. I looked into the soul of my Meme's eyes and felt the deep joy and love of a moment in time. I saw the smile she had on her birthday and felt the intense love that she had for me.

I saw into each person's soul, and in between, I would feel and hear the thunder of the wings as I was pulled higher and higher. Every frame was a happy or sad moment in time for someone in my past. In every frame, each person's face I looked upon would bring me deep into an emotion I gave to them. It seemed like it went on forever. I was pulled higher and higher.

There were many eyes on the wheels; they kept going and going. I felt intense sadness, happiness, grief, love, hatred, joy, pity, madness, and wonder. All of these emotions tirelessly went back and forth, and I saw different faces and eyes. This was the most exhausting thing I ever had to go through. I believe that this is a purification one needs to undergo to enter the kingdom of heaven.

All of a sudden, I was alone in the darkness. As it hovered all around, panic began to set in. I stood there, frozen, with my eyes carefully searching for any sign of life. The very essence of this atmosphere began to come alive. There was a long tunnel made of dark amethyst stones. As I gazed into the distance, I saw a faint, small flicker of light. I felt a presence touching my right hand. I looked on my right, and there was a woman next to me. She took my hand, not touching but holding it. I felt a covering of peace embrace my body in a strange but familiar way. I knew this woman would keep me safe as we gracefully flowed to an unknown destination.

A satisfying, comforting feeling washed over me. I began to look all around. The deep purple walls began to glisten with vitality. To my amazement, the shimmering hues began to take on a form of their very own. As we slowly moved, I could see walls ahead on the left and right, with sounds coming from both sides. As we drew closer, I could see dark holes within the walls. I could feel the arms of discontentment reaching out toward us. I tried to look for faces but could only hear the slight sounds of mourning, lost souls crying out from behind the walls. My heart felt a deep sense of sorrow for the souls who seemed so distressed.

Without fear, I looked to my right at the woman beside me. She was very beautiful and angelic in her appearance. She had long, dark, wavy hair and pale white skin. She was dressed in a white flowing gown and had dark brown eyes and red lips. She reminded me of my Aunty Anita who had committed suicide when I was a child. We walked, but it was not like walking on earth. We flowed together through this place. I started to notice the small flicker of light in the distance.

As we slowly drew closer to this light, it became apparent that this would be my final destination. My entire concentration was now focused and intrigued by this light. The intensity of this light began to magnify and consume us. I felt an intense love and immeasurable peace all around me. When I looked to my right, the beautiful, angelic woman was gone.

I was encompassed in this glorious light. I glanced out in the distance, and I could see a woman in a silky smooth, shining white robe. The closer and more encompassed I became, the more it became clear. There I stood, ten feet away from my Meme. The light was extremely bright and translucent; yet it did not hurt my eyes. The intensity of the all-consuming power and glory of the light of God came rushing from behind my Meme and poured right into me. This awesome powerful light of God encompassed above, below, and all around us.

I felt like I was wrapped in the arms of a most powerful God, and I felt a strong, unconditional love of God holding us both still in this place. This holy presence of God penetrated my innermost being—mind, heart, body, and soul. I stood there, unable to move, with an intense, euphoric feeling of just being.

There she was, my Meme, the most influential person in my life. She was the woman who taught me about the Bible, the Trinity, how to live, and how to die. She was the woman who was always there for me when I needed her and who I adored the most in my life. There she was, standing right in front of me. The last time I saw her, she was sick with cancer and dying in a bed in her living room. She was completely healed and more beautiful than I could even imagine as she stood there in her long, white, flowing gown. She was smiling with her arms wide open. The preeminence of God flowed through her into me.

Revelation 21:4–5 says,

> "And God will wipe away every tear from their eyes, there shall be no more death, nor sorrow, nor crying. There shall be no more pain, for the former things passed away." Then He who sat on the throne

said, "Behold, I make all things new." And He said
to me, "Write, for these words are true and faithful."

As I stood in the holy presence of God's light, I had no human
emotions or concerns. There were no thoughts of anyone on earth.
I was just entranced, enthralled, and consumed with complete
abandonment in the light of God in the heavens with my Meme.
The only thought I had was to remain in this place with Meme
completely healed, forever. She had no pain, sickness, sorrow, or
death; she was healed and would forever live in the kingdom of
God. This was the purest form of tranquility and most extreme,
passionate love that one could ever imagine. I had no desire for
earthly things; I just wanted to dwell in this place forever.

Her entire being was purified by the light of God. Her hair
was as white as snow, and a crown of gold was upon her head.
Her face glowed with the love of God. Her arms stretched out to
the sides as she welcomed me in. There we were, secured together
in the light of God. Her eyes sparkled and beamed with gladness;
her smile was filled with life and joy. Her beauty projected the
preeminence of God.

As I basked in the radiance, I said, "Meme, I love you." But it
was not like speaking here on earth. We talked to each other but
not out loud. We were communicating in a heavenly language
within the Spirit of God.

Meme said, "I love you, too." It was incredible to see her there,
healed, smiling at me, beaming even more than when I could walk
through her door such a long, long time ago.

Again, I said, "Meme, I love you."

Then she said, "I love you, too. It's not your time."

I said, "But Meme, I love you."

Again she said, "It's not your time; you have to go back and
do good things on earth."

I said, "No, Meme. I love you. I don't want to go."

Yet again, she said, "It's not your time." And this supernatural
experience was done.

CHAPTER 6

Bittersweet Recovery

I woke up for just a moment to hear the sound of sirens above me. I cried out in pain from the bumpy ride of the ambulance and then slipped out of consciousness.

I woke up a second time for a moment, feeling a cold solution being pouring out on my skinless back. I heard, "You're in the hospital, and we're putting solution on your back right now to get the dirt and glass out." I was in agony and started crying and screaming in pain, and then I slipped out of consciousness again.

The next time I woke up, it was a few days later. I saw my family all around me and couldn't understand why they all looked so worried. My Aunt Mary had her hand on my shoulder and said, "You're our miracle child. You're alive." She was crying. I saw my brother walk out of the room, wiping a tear from his eye. My father, mother, daughter, sister, and Aunty Mary stood around me. I thought I was at some kind of family gathering, and I couldn't understand why they were sad. Of course, with all the morphine I was on, I couldn't feel the pain I was in.

I noticed the sounds of machines around me and realized I must have been hurt pretty badly but really didn't know what condition I was in. For a little while, I saw all their faces and then slipped out of consciousness again.

I woke up in the middle of the night. *Am I dreaming?* There was a man in my room, and I felt uneasy and afraid. He came in to give me more medicine through my machine; I dozed off and woke up some time the next day.

I finally realized I was not dreaming but really in the hospital. My mom and dad brought Laura to see me. I asked them what happened and how I got there. They told me I was in a bad accident, and it was going to be a long recovery. I told them that the hospital was creepy; there was a man in there the previous night. They told me it was okay; it was just a male nurse. I asked my dad to ask someone in the hospital if they would let my daughter or someone stay with me overnight. My daughter wanted to stay with me for the weekend, so she slept in the bed next to me.

As I went in and out of consciousness, I noticed people here and there. Only my father, mother, and daughter were there at certain times. I became more aware of my condition. It did not look good. I had a neck brace that I called the Dr. Spock brace. It went all around the back and on both sides of my head and had a piece that went halfway down my back. I had a huge hip brace that went from my waist down past my knee; it had an uncomfortable silver bar on it.

My body was swollen from the left top of my head to my left foot. I could not move, and the nurses came in three times a day to clean glass out of me. There was a lot of glass and dirt.

I'll never forget the pain of them pouring a solution on me and scrubbing the glass and dirt out. I just lay there as the cloth scraped across my skin, back and forth, and all I could think was, *Is this ever going to end? When is this nurse going to stop? I can't take it anymore!* My sister later told me that my back had no skin on it. She watched as one nurse showed the others how to be careful when moving me and changing my bandages. After many tests, they found out that I had a fractured back, fractured neck, dislocated hip, and left traumatic brain injury.

A lawyer came in to assess the situation with his coworker. He had his coworker take pictures of my body and they asked me some questions about the accident. Then he asked me, *If there was anything you could have right now, what would you want?* I said that I wanted to go home. He worked on it for some time; I don't recall how long.

They put a hospital bed in my living room; I had nurses around the clock and someone to come in for half a day to clean, cook, and do household chores. It felt terrible to have to lie in a hospital bed, watching strange people I didn't even know come and go from my house. I took about thirty-nine pills a day and lay there, helpless, wondering if I would be wheelchair-bound or in that bed forever.

Many questions ran through my head as I lay there. *Will I be able to walk again? How will I be able to take care of my daughter? Will she be okay? Will I ever be able to work again? What about the heavens and Meme? What did this all mean?* I couldn't even walk; I just lay there, helpless and powerless over my situation. *Am I going to die?*

Psalm 42:5 says, "Why are you cast down, O my soul? And why are you disquieted within me? Hope in God, for I shall yet praise Him for the help of His countenance."

I was at home on a hospital bed in my living room. The only way I could get back and forth to the hospital was if my dad drove me. I needed to drive in a smooth-riding car; any bump I felt would cause extreme pain.

After being home three weeks, I had an appointment to go to the hospital, and the doctor gave me a checkup and had x-rays done of my neck and back. When the x-rays came up, he said, "There's no way these could be hers. They must have made a mistake. Send her back down again for more". So they took me down for more x-rays and brought them back. He was perplexed.

He said, "This is impossible. It would take twelve weeks to six months for her bones to heal this fast."

I told him, "I was in the light of God, and that's why my bones are healed so quickly." I didn't quite understand how God did this or who this God really was, but the physical healing was there. The doctor couldn't believe it. My dad and I couldn't believe it. We were all in a bit of a shock at this miracle. Then my dad shook his head and said, "Yeah, she had a near-death experience. She died in the car accident and was sent back." The doctor looked perplexed, shook his head, and left to attend to his other patients.

But there was something very different about my presence. Before the accident, I kept my life busy at all times and lived in the fast lane. I was an adrenaline junkie; I never wanted to miss a thing. Then, after being in the light, my presence was very calm and mellow. I listened more and did not talk so fast.

I believe God just slowed me down so I could hear His voice, even though at the time, I had no idea it was in fact God's voice. Even my dad, my daughter, and others who knew me noticed there was something very different about me. My mind was crystal clear and at peace, and I carried peace within myself. This is the peace I had searched for my whole life. Something was very different, and I often thought of Meme and the light. Having so much time to ponder this experience and how it was so much bigger than me, and how blessed I was to lay in God's presence.

I lay in my living room, and my daughter put pictures of my horse and family on the wall next to me, giving me hope and determination to walk again. Slowly, I started to get out of bed and make it all the way down the hallway and back. My life consisted of going to doctors' appointments and getting exercise with my walker, going down the hallway and back. All my so-called friends didn't even come to visit me. My best friend did not call or even visit once. She was too busy having a love affair with her alcohol. The only people who were there for me now were my family.

I spent nights out at the pub with all my so-called friends. It's amazing that when it all went down and tragedy struck my life, they were still sitting in the same old bar stools, drinking with the same old crowd. These people I'd known for years couldn't care less about me. They didn't even call me. I was at peace with myself but also had mixed emotions and felt all alone, lying in my hospital bed day after day.

At my next doctor's visit, they decided to give me a test to find out if I needed to have hip surgery. They injected my left hip area with sixteen dye-filled needles all at once and put me into the MRI machine to see what was happening. The doctors then found out that when they first positioned and snapped my hip together after the accident, it was done wrong. They now had to go in, dislocate it, scrape it out, and put it back together again. They said there was only a 40 percent chance that I would walk again. I had nothing to lose, so they made an appointment for me.

The surgery was planned for a month and a half from that time. I dreaded the surgery, and at the same time, I wanted to just get it over with. A week and a half went by, and I received a call from the doctor's office. They said another surgery had been cancelled for tomorrow. "If you can come on such short notice, we can give this appointment to you." I took them up on the offer and was back in the hospital the next day. I had the hip surgery done. It was a great success. It only took a week until I was back up and walking with my walker.

I had to laugh because my Meme said I was going to go back to the earth to do good things. I thought, *How in the heck I am going to do this in this condition?* God was certainly looking out for me and healing me more and more with each passing day.

As the weeks went on, I was walking with my cane and going to doctors' appointments every week. After months went by, I finally got to take a real shower! What an incredible experience that was. I was very grateful for hot water, soap, and washing my hair with real shampoo—standing in my shower, no less. The things that we take for granted every day completely amaze me. I am now grateful for everything I have, even the little things most people take for granted.

One day, my dad and I were chatting at my kitchen table. I told him that I wished he and my mom were in Texas. This way, I could take a break from my new reality of life and visit them. You see, during the spring, summer, they were in New England and in the fall and winter, they went to Texas. So my dad said, "Why don't you go to Aunty Noreen's house for a visit?"

I thought to myself, *That would be awesome!* I said to my dad, "I don't have a doctor's appointment for about three and a half weeks."

He asked, "When do you want to go?"

Kidding around, I said, "Tomorrow."

My dad left and said, "Goodbye. I love you. I'll call you soon."

That night, I received a phone call from my father. He said, "Pack up your bags; you're leaving for Aunty Noreen's tomorrow. I'll pick you up at three and take you to the airport." So the next day, my cane and I were on our way to Aunty Noreen's in the beautiful, state of Texas.

CHAPTER 7

Jesus in My Heart

I arrived at Aunty Noreen's house on a Monday. I was exhausted from the plane ride, but it was great to see her smiling face! Aunty Noreen was a lot like my dad. She was fun to be around, and I loved her great smile and huge, loving hugs! As a matter of fact, we had a lot in common. My middle name is Noreen. My birthday is on November 22, and hers is November 24. We are fifteen years apart in age, and fifteen years before I arrived in Texas, she took Jesus Christ to be her Lord and Savior. I was in the home of a Christian woman, getting hugs and kisses with the love of God. I thanked God she hadn't changed or lost her sense of humor and that she was still a lot of fun to be around.

It was nice being in Texas and very relaxing. The sun was shining, and I spent a lot of time resting and talking with Aunty Noreen. Meme was Aunty Noreen's mother and my dad's sister. Aunty Noreen was the baby of her family, and so was I—another thing we had in common. I told her about my near-death experience, seeing Meme, and how she sent me back. I told her I was tired of the way things were and how I didn't know what to do about it. She told me all about God and said that if I put God first, everything would fall into place.

During our talks throughout the week, I had many concerns about not being able to do all the things I used to. How was I going to work, take care of my daughter, or even clean my house? Aunty Noreen kept telling me not to worry; God would take care of it. If you put God first, everything else will fall into place. She noticed a change in me—she felt a peaceful, healing presence coming from me. It was the presence of God coming from my experience. It was great to be there, even though she kept talking about church and God.

As it got closer to Friday, she kept telling me about her church and how nice everyone was. She said it wasn't like other churches. She talked about Pastor Paul, her brothers and sisters in Christ, and how it was like one big family. She told me that I should go with her and that everyone who lived in her house had to go to church. I told her that I wasn't going to church; I was in the light of God, and I was all set with that. There was no way some preacher was going to brainwash me and tell me what to do in with my life.

Aunty Noreen kept talking about how there was a band at church and that because I was a musician, I would really like it. She told me they put the words up on a screen, I could sing along, and I would really like the music. She said I didn't have to sit, kneel, or stand like before. When the service started, everybody stood up and sang, and then I could sit down for the rest of the service. I kept telling her that I was all set. "I'm sure it works for you, Aunty, but if you don't mind, I will just stay here."

Sunday morning came around, and Aunty Noreen tried to wake me up for church. She said, "Sarah, do you want to go to church today? We're leaving in about a half an hour."

I said, "No, Aunty; you just go," and I rolled over and tried to go back to sleep.

Twenty minutes later, Aunty Noreen came back in my room and said, "We're leaving for church in ten minutes; if you're not ready, we're leaving without you."

I said, "Okay, Aunty. I'm good with that."

Then Aunty said, "Okay, you just stay here all day by yourself. There's going to be a cookout after church, and we won't be home till at least four, so you just stay here *all by yourself, all day long*, and we'll see you when we get back."

I thought about being all alone in my aunt's house by myself all day and said, "Wait, I'm coming." I was tired of being alone, lying around the house, and doing nothing, and the last thing I wanted was to be at Aunty Noreen's doing the same thing all day. So I got ready as fast as I could, found my good clothes, washed up quick, got in the car, and was on my way to church.

We were walking toward the church, and I saw people at the door hugging people and saying hi. I'd never seen anything like that before. We got to the door, and a big, jolly gentleman handed me a flyer with a smile and said, "And what's your name, young lady?"

Of course, I said, "Sarah."

He said, "Well, enjoy the service today. God bless you." Then he asked, "Is she with you, Noreen?"

Aunty Noreen said, "Yes, that's my niece. She's visiting." He laughed because Aunty Noreen always brought new people to church. Aunty Noreen had her own section.

One day, Pastor Paul said, "Who is this, Noreen? Could you please stand up?" She stood up. Pastor Paul said, "It's nice to finally meet you." He learned that she would pick up all the people at the campground where she worked and bring them to church. Pastor Paul had an old bus—a really old bus with an old stick shift. He gave it to her to pick people up. My cousins did not want to be seen on this bus, but I got a kick out of riding on it with Aunty Noreen. We laughed when we rode that bus. She's an amazing woman of God.

The church service started, and the music began to play. With the words up on the screen, I could follow along and sing, just like Aunty Noreen said. There was a lady named Paula on the right side of me; she was Aunty Noreen's friend. Aunty Noreen was on my left side. I started singing the songs with the worship team, and my whole body shook. Paula sounded like an angel singing next to me. I felt great inside, just like a little piece of the light of God.

"Come to Me, all you who labor and are heavy laden, and I will give you rest. Take my yoke upon you and learn from Me for I am gentle and lowly in heart and you will find rest for your souls. For my yoke is easy and my burden is light" (Matthew 11:28–30).

I started to cry, and my body shook. I had no idea what was happening to me. Aunty Noreen went to get me some Kleenex. I kept crying and shaking. I heard a beautiful voice singing next to me; it felt like I had my own angel singing just for me. I said to Aunty Noreen, "What's happening to me? Why am I crying and shaking?"

She said, "it's okay, Sarah," and she was smiling. She got me some more Kleenex. I wept harder, and Aunty Noreen went to get me some more Kleenex. Then a man told her, "Noreen, take the whole box, please!" (This later turned into a Kleenex joke).

Pastor Paul started to preach the Word of God, and I felt like I was the only one in the room and he was talking just to me. He started talking about all who are tired and weary in this life. Take the yoke of God upon you, and He will give you rest. Nobody has to go through this life alone, but with the Lord Jesus Christ as your Savior, all things are possible. God created us in His image, and He wants to fill us with peace, love, and joy.

Pastor Paul talked about all the things that Aunty Noreen and I discussed all week long, and I felt like he was talking just to me and that Aunty Noreen must have told him everything we talked about. How could she? I turned to Aunty Noreen and asked, "Did you tell him everything we talked about?"

She said, "No," laughing.

I said, "You did too!"

And she said, "No, I didn't. Sarah, just listen."

At the end of the message, Pastor Paul said, "If anyone who doesn't know Jesus Christ as their Savior and wants to know Him and follow Him, you can come up here and say a simple prayer with me." The heels of my feet started lifting up, as if my body was going to walk up there, and I kept pushing them down. I asked Aunty Noreen, "What is happening to me?"

She laughed and said, "It's okay. It's just the Holy Spirit. It's okay, Sarah" A woman went up and made an announcement that she forgot at the beginning of the service. I thought, *Phew! I don't have to go up there now!* Then after the woman was done, Pastor Paul again asked, "Is there anyone who would like to start a new life and take Jesus to be your Savior?"

My heels came up, and my body went right up to the stage. I fell down on my knees and started crying. This was totally out of character for me. I didn't know anyone besides my aunt, and the Holy Spirit moved me up to the stage. I said, "I'm a sinner, and I want to take Jesus to be my Savior. It's so dark at home that I don't know what I'm going to do."

At this time, Pastor Paul led me through the sinner's prayer. "Dear Father God in heaven, I come to You in the name of Jesus. I am a sinner, and I am very sorry for my sins and the life that I have lived. I need Your help and forgiveness, God. I believe that Jesus Christ died on the cross and shed His precious blood for my sins."

"If we confess the Lord our God and believe in our hearts that God raised Jesus from the dead, we shall be saved" (Romans 10:9).

"Right now, I confess Jesus Christ as the Lord of my soul. With my heart, I believe that God raised Jesus from the dead. This very moment, I accept Jesus Christ into my heart as my own personal Savior, and according to His Word, right now I am saved. I just want to thank you, Jesus, for dying for me and giving me life. Amen."

I took Jesus Christ to be my Savior and asked to be forgiven of all my sins. I now believed that Jesus died and rose again from the grave. I am written in the Lamb's book and given everlasting life with my heavenly Father. I have brothers and sisters in Christ all over the world, and I am now saved in God's arms forever.

"Jesus said: 'Most assuredly, I say to you, unless one is born again, he cannot see the kingdom of God'" (John 3:3).

My body was still shaking in the Spirit. Pastor Paul told me to stand just to the right of him. Then another girl came up, said the sinner's prayer, and took Jesus Christ to be her Savior. I was still shaking in the Holy Spirit. Then Pastor Paul had all of the people in the congregation come up to meet their new sisters in Christ.

It all felt surreal, like a dream. I did not go to this church and did not know anyone there. But the Holy Spirit hit me, and God touched my heart; I was never to be the same again.

God sent His Son, Jesus, to die on the cross for us sinners. He came to heal the brokenhearted and give sinners everlasting life. All we have to do is to repent. If you want to repent of your sins and take Jesus Christ to be your Savior, He will be there for you no matter how bad you think your situation is. It is by God's grace, which is an undeserved gift, and through His mercy that we are saved. We don't deserve this. He is an awesome, holy God.

At the picnic, I met all Aunty Noreen's friends, or sisters and brothers in Christ, and Paula, and I started talking. I said "Paula, you have such a beautiful, angelic voice! I could listen to you sing forever!"

Then Paula says to me in her southern accent, "Sarah, you must be talking about someone else. Darlin', I can't sing a lick." Right then, I knew that God had opened the heavens, and the angels were singing over her. There were open heavens over that church on that day, and when someone comes to Christ, the angels in heaven rejoice. They were rejoicing over us. I love it when the heavens open and you can hear the choir of heaven.

After the picnic was over, we went back to Aunty Noreen's house. I was still shaking in the Spirit for about another two hours. What a beautiful and blessed day!

The next day, Aunty Noreen took me shopping and bought me an easy-to-read Bible that I could understand. She told me to start in the New Testament with Matthew and not to read Revelation, then go to the Old Testament in Genesis, and then read Revelation last. So of course, still being a little defiant, I read Revelation first, then the Old Testament next, and then the New Testament. I had to do it my way. I couldn't get my face out of the Bible and read it night and day. I read through different parts of it once and reread some more. It was like I couldn't get enough of the Word of God in me. Whatever this was, I wanted more.

I heard that Aunty Noreen's church was on the last day of a two-week study on the prayer Our Father. I asked Pastor Paul if his wife could give me a two-day crash course on it, and she did. She gave me all the paperwork, and I did all the homework. First, I learned the meaning of the prayer Our Father; I later lived it out.

There was only one more weekend to go in Texas. I decided that before I went home, I needed to be baptized because New England wasn't like Texas, meaning Texas is close to the Bible belt. When you go to the grocery store or to a restaurant, most people will say, "God bless you; have a nice day!" Where I lived, it was very dark, and a relationship with Jesus is a necessity that is lacking.

Aunty Noreen called Pastor Paul and asked him if he would baptize me in her pool on Sunday after church. He said, "Noreen, you know it's a long weekend. There's not going to be enough people; a lot of people are going away."

Of course, Aunty Noreen said to him, "How many people do you need, Pastor Paul? This is Noreen you're talking to; if you need fifty, I'll get them."

Pastor Paul laughed and said, "You only need two or more to be gathered in His name. I'll do it."

During the week, Aunty Noreen kept saying to me, "What are you going to do about that live-in boyfriend of yours? You know he's got to go. You can't live in sin." The entire first week I was there, Aunty said to me, "All you have to do is put God first, and He will take care of everything; don't you worry."

My response to her was, "Aunty Noreen, don't worry about it. God's going to take care of everything; don't you know?"

She said, "I know, but you can't live like that anymore."

Aunty Noreen had been having a problem with the pool for a few weeks. We hadn't been able to swim in it because it was a greenish color. She called pool guys to fix it when I first arrived, and nothing happened. The next day, she tried to use chemicals, and nothing happened. As the days went on, the pool was still green. I asked her if I could get baptized in a lake. But there were already too many people coming and bringing food. She said, "They're not going to want to go all the way to the lake just to come all the way back here; it would just be too much. By the time you get baptized and we eat, people will be able to decide if they want to stick around or leave. So it looks like you're getting dunked in a green pool."

I thought to myself, *Great*.

This was the beginning of the first three miracles. The night before the baptism, Aunty Noreen spread her hands out over the pool. Almost kidding, she said, "Lord, you parted the Red Sea; you've raised the dead. Now I'm asking you to please, please make this pool clean." The next day, we woke up, and the pool water was sparkling clean. We couldn't believe it. God did a miracle!

After church, we got ready for the baptism. I had an old friend, Sam, who lived in Texas come to my baptism. I walked around, asking my Aunty if she or anyone had seen Sam. No one knew where he was. Then the second miracle happened. My Aunty said, "Come over here. Go look on the kitchen table to see what Sam brought for you."

I looked on the kitchen table and found three long-stemmed yellow roses in a vase. I yelled, "Look, Meme's here! Meme's here! And what made me think she wouldn't show up on a special day such as this?"

Sam said, "I'm sorry. I tried to get white roses for your baptism for purity, and I went to three different places, and this was all I could find." He had no idea what the yellow roses represented to us.

I ran next door to my Cousin Anna's house and said, "Come and look who's here."

She asked, "What?"

I said, "Come, look who came to my baptism. You won't believe it!"

She thought I was about half crazy and out of my mind. Then she followed me into the kitchen and said, "Oh my, Meme's here!"

Matthew 28:18–20 says,

> Then Jesus came and spoke to them, saying, "All authority has been given to Me in heaven and on earth. Go therefore and make disciples of all the nations, baptizing them in the name of the Father and the Son and of the Holy Spirit, teaching them to observe all things that I have commanded you; and lo, I am with you always, even to the end of the age." Amen.

Pastor Paul baptized me in the pool, and about thirty-five people came. They brought food and played music; we sang to the Lord and had a wonderful time of fellowship. For the first time since the accident, I didn't have just a clear mind, my mind, heart, and soul also became one with Christ, and I felt complete. How awesome and almighty is He! How great is our God who can put together so many things, showing us that He is right there with us. The three long-stemmed yellow roses signified my Meme's presence. And God made sure that the pool was clean. I love you, Lord. You're an awesome God, pure and true!

After everyone ate and most people headed home, a few of my new sisters in Christ took me aside and told me to say a few syllables like "ba" and "sa," and soon I was speaking in tongues.

This is a way to pray to God in a special language so that nothing comes between you and God.

At the time, I felt completely strange with this prayer language coming out of my mouth. I went from being an atheist who didn't go to church to praying to God in what God's Word calls tongues. The good thing was that after my near-death experience, I felt different inside. Because I'd taken the Lord Jesus Christ to be my Savior, my heart and soul felt peaceful and one with God.

After everyone had left, my cousins and I sat around talking by the pool. I received a phone call. The third miracle of the day was about to happen. My daughter was on the phone, saying to me, "Mom, are you sitting down? I have something to tell you."

I said, "Yeah, I'm sitting down. What?"

She asked, "Are you sure you're sitting down?"

I said, "Laura, just tell me."

She said, "Mom, I don't know how to tell you this, but guess who is packing his things, and he's moving out."

I shouted out, "Praise God! Praise God!" My daughter thought that I'd be upset, but instead I cried out with pure joy. "I told you, Aunty. I told you God would take care of it. He's moving out!" My daughter was relieved that I wasn't upset and started to laugh with me. When we let God take care of things and trust in Him, He will answer all our prayers, especially when they keep us on the right path. Thank you, Lord, that you answer our prayers in your time.

It was my last day with Aunty Noreen. We had breakfast together at our favorite spot near the lake before she took me to the airport. I thanked her for all she did for me. She said that there's nothing more fulfilling in this world than having someone come to the Lord. She said it was her pleasure and let the glory be to God! Now it was time to board the plane with my cane, Bible in hand, and head off to New England.

CHAPTER 8

Full Circle

I arrived home, in a little town in New England. I wanted to find a church but had no idea on where to start. So I took my Aunty Noreen's advice and prayed about it. All week, I prayed to God and asked Him where I should to go to church.

I didn't want to go to Deerfield Church, in the town I lived and partied in. I thought that people would know me, and they probably wouldn't let me in. There's only one bar in town, and I was barred for life for fighting. I had my name right up there on the wall with a note saying not to let me in.

I decided to look in the phone book and found a church in a nearby town. I put on my best dress and went off to church. I walked in, sat down, and there was no one to greet me; no one even spoke to me at all. The service was not what I expected. I really couldn't feel the Holy Spirit in the house.

The next week, I kept praying to God as to what church I should attend. I felt like the Holy Spirit was pulling me toward Deerfield Church. Pulling into the parking lot was really hard for me; I struggled getting out of my car. When I walked into the church, I didn't know what to expect. To my surprise, I was greeted with a smile and a hug from Pastor Rudy. As he handed me a flyer, he said, "Good morning, sister." (He always said it with an accent: "Sista.")

I said, "Good morning," went in, and sat down.

This was a small country church that was built a long time ago. It was lovely and quaint; I felt very comfortable and liked it a lot. The music started playing, and the old hymns began to play. These hymns are still very close to my heart. The words were up on the wall on the left side, right where I was sitting. I began to sing along. The church was rocking, and everyone sang to the Lord, even Pastor Rick. I can still picture his face. He was filled with the Holy Spirit as he sang to the Lord. I found my new church home.

Because of my near-death experience, I thought that God had taken away my alcoholism. I had no ambition or thoughts of drinking at the time. Then one night, I received a phone call from my ex-boyfriend. I had not seen him since he moved out. He had to go to court for the accident because we were both drinking. They blamed him for the accident. I still don't believe it was his fault. He asked me to go with him, and being the good Christian woman I was, I wanted to help him.

I decided to meet him for dinner so we could talk. We went to a country lounge not far away, a place I used to ride my horse to. I would have a couple of drinks with those who I thought were friends.

My motives were good; I was just going to have a burger and a soda, find out what was going on, and leave. An old friend came over and asked me to do a shot with her. I first said no. She put one in front of me, and I ended up drinking something like eleven beers and fourteen shots of Jack Daniels. My ex-boyfriend gave me a ride home.

I woke up feeling like a sinner. I had no business being in a bar, drinking, especially with all the medicine I was taking for pain. I woke up for the first time since receiving Jesus and felt the truth of my alcohol problem. My head was pounding, and I felt sick inside. I just wanted to crawl into a hole. Someone who had been in some trouble before with alcohol came to mind. I remembered a conversation we had about some meetings he went to for alcohol abuse. I found out there was one near my house on Monday night and planned to attend.

I went to church that Sunday. It was very hard for me to walk up those stairs; I felt like such a sinner! How could I drink like that and then go to church in the holy presence of God? Well, I did. I went into church, and during worship, I asked God for forgiveness for drinking.

I could not believe that the sermon was about excessive drinking and how it can keep you far away from God. If you want to have a pure relationship with Him, you never do anything to excess. The minister spoke about how to be a good Christian by putting on Christ and not doing anything to harm your body. We are temples; God dwells inside us. I was blessed to hear what God had to say to me through Pastor Rick—now more than ever. God wants to meet with us even in the middle of our messes!

> And do this, knowing the time, that now it is high time to awake out of sleep; for now our salvation is nearer than we first believed. The night is far spent, the day is at hand. Therefore let us cast off the works of darkness, and let us put on the armor of light. Let us walk properly, as in the day, not in revelry and drunkenness, not in lewdness and lust, not in strife and envy. But put on the Lord Jesus Christ, and make no provision for the flesh, to fulfill its lusts. (Romans 13:11–14)

On Monday night, I decided to go to this support group. That night I learned that I was an alcoholic. It was the worst and best day of my life. I believe that God has to bring us to our knees or let us hit our bottoms so we can learn how to rise up and change the way we live. He wants to unravel what has been taught to us until we become undone. This way, God can fill us and reteach us how to live our new lives. We can learn to live lives of change, repentance, forgiveness, and freedom by reading God's Word and following His Son, Jesus Christ.

I never drank every day, but I partied on the weekends like a rock star. I always thought that alcoholics were people wearing trench coats—beggars out on the streets with no place to live. When I looked around the room, I saw people from all walks of life. That night, I heard a testimony of a woman who spoke of what it was like to be a weekend warrior alcoholic. She said something that made complete sense to me. She said that it's not when you drink or how many days you drink but what happens when you drink.

Even though I did not drink every day, I was like her, a weekend warrior. When I did drink, my life was out of control, and I was powerless over alcohol. I still wondered at the beginning of this meeting if I was in the right place. After hearing this woman's testimony, I knew for sure that I was an alcoholic. Once again, God brought me to the meeting where I could identify with someone who was like me.

I attended these meetings regularly. This is how I met my sponsor, best friend, and soon-to-be sister in Christ, Naomi. She brought me through steps of my life that helped me to grow into a greater woman of God—who He created me to be. I would not carry the baggage from my past around with me. She also taught me how to live in the real world and introduced me to the right people. She brought me out of the steps of my own hell and into the steps of truly walking with God and living a good life— walking the walk and talking the talk.

God has blessed me with this woman in my life. She took many hours out of her life to bless my life. I found out what it was like to be truly open and honest, let go of the past, and walk in the present in the presence of God.

My daughter was confused about this new "God" and "church" thing. I believe she liked that I was happy, going to church, and mostly that I had stopped drinking, but at the same time, she was rebellious toward the new mom she had. She sometimes wanted her old mom back—the one who used to be normal and not talk about God and church all the time.

We went through some difficult times together, and she moved in with her father for a while, thinking that his rules would be easier than mine. His rules ended up being stricter, and she went back and forth between the two houses a few times. I knew that God was in control and would take care of everything. I prayed for her every day, and even though we disagreed, she was always the sunshine of my life!

I was still going to doctors at least two or three times a month and walking with my cane. All I had to do was to read my Bible, go to church, and go to meetings. I joined a women's Bible study on Tuesday mornings at ten. I kept to myself, went to my new Bible study, read God's Word every day, and played some of the new Christian music I heard.

One day after church, there was a church picnic outside. A lady from church asked me if I was going to the picnic. Her mother used to work for me at a restaurant I used to own. I said, "No thank you; I'm not really hungry." The truth was that I was keeping to myself and not sure how to have relationships with people. I sometimes felt like I had nothing in common with these people except for the love of God.

I was always in His Word and worshiped Him on my own when I wasn't at church. I read a lot of books and my Bible. I couldn't get enough, and I always studied the lessons preached on Sunday and in Bible study. I never had a normal life like people who went to church, whatever that looks like.

This woman said, "My mom's coming. She won't come to church, but she always comes to the picnic for the food."

I said, "Jenny Mama's coming?" This was my nickname for her.

She said, "Yes, my mom's coming. You should stay. She'd love to see you."

Needless to say, I decided to stay for the picnic so I could see my "Jenny Mama". It was a beautiful day. The sun was shining, and I felt it was time to do something. I went to get a soda and noticed that everyone was dressed casually because of the picnic. There was a pavilion behind the church. Children played games, and there were men working hard, cooking lots of hotdogs and burgers on the grill. Women got the side dishes, salads, and desserts ready. There was music playing in the background, and you could feel the love in the fellowship of the brothers and sisters in Christ. Everyone was just having a relaxed, good old time.

I sat down at a picnic table where I didn't know anyone. There were people sitting across the table from me, a woman sitting to my right, and no one to my left. Everyone was talking about things going on in their lives. All of a sudden, Judy, a lady from my Bible study, came and sat next to me. She was a tiny little thing with dark brown hair and lots of energy! She probably weighed about ninety-five pounds and was always filled with an overabundance of the joy of the Lord.

Judy said, "How are you doing today, Sarah? It's good to see you out at the picnic."

I said, "I'm doing fine; it's a beautiful day."

We made small talk, and then she asked me, "So, how is it that you came to the Lord?"

I said, "Well, I was hit by a Mack truck on the highway, had a near-death experience, and took Jesus to be my Savior when I was in Texas."

A lady sitting next to me had light brown, shoulder-length hair, brown eyes, and a nice, warm smile. She looked like someone I could hang out with. She wore sneakers, jeans, and a nice shirt. She asked me, "You were hit by a Mack truck on the highway?"

I said, "Yes."

She asked me, "When did this happen?"

I said, "November 15, 2000."

She asked, "Did it happen on Highway 202?"

I said, "Yes," wondering how she would know that.

Then she asked, "Did it happen on Exit 7?"

I said, "Yes."

She then started crying and hugging me, saying, "You're alive; you're alive. Your hair—I remember the color of your hair. I can't believe it. You're alive."

We cried and held each other for a few minutes. I asked her, "Did you work for the ambulance? Did you save my life?"

For a while longer, she just kept saying, "You're alive. I remember the color of your hair. You're alive."

After we both calmed down, I found out that her name was Joan and her husband's name was Ken. On the night the accident happened at around 9:40 p.m., they were going to stop at a store but decided not to. She was following her husband home. As Ken got off the exit, she saw that he almost hit something that was in the triangle part of the exit. As she came up behind him, she saw a body lying there. She began to flash her lights and beep her horn so he would stop. They both pulled over to the side of the road, and she called the ambulance. She said there was a Mack truck on the side of the highway and a smashed-up SUV thirty feet away from my body.

They got out of their cars and walked toward my body. The closer they came, the more apparent the details of my appearance were. She said it was gross; I was covered in glass and blood. She couldn't even make out what my face looked like. My left leg was dislocated and up underneath my head; the only thing she could recognize was my long, strawberry blonde hair. Ken said, "You know what we have to do."

She said, "I can't; it's too bloody and gross." He put their coats over my body so they could pray for my healing and salvation.

She said I wasn't breathing or moving, but they just kept on praying. Then Ken went to check if anyone else was hurt. He saw my roommate in the car, and he seemed to be okay. Ken saw that I was about thirty feet away from the totaled SUV I had been in. Then he came back to pray for me with Joan.

Because of the near-death experience I had, I asked her about how long I lay there, not moving or breathing. She said I wasn't moving or breathing for about fifteen minutes. After that, the ambulance came. The paramedics asked Joan and Ken if they were family, and they said no. Then the paramedics asked Ken and Joan if they were involved in the accident, and they said no. They were told, "If you're not part of this accident and you're not family, you need to leave immediately." At that moment, Joan saw one of my fingers start to move.

We became friends. To this day, I call them my angels on earth. I believe that if I had died that night, I would have gone straight to hell. Their prayers for my healing and salvation brought me back so I could have a second chance to take Jesus to be my Lord and Savior. I now know that when I die, I will be in heaven. I will get to see my Meme again. I will be walking in the garden with Jesus and singing with the angels around the throne of God for all eternity.

Joan and I started to spend some time together. She later told me that Ken's faith had not been as strong as it used to be. Now that he witnessed this miracle, he knew that his prayers were answered. This restored his faith completely. He was back on his knees again, praying and pressing into God more than he had ever before. God will never let anything snatch us out of His hands. He will always come through in His timing. He always shows us that He is with us, sometimes using incredible, supernatural things to get our attention. What are the chances of me meeting the people who were praying over my dead body a year after the accident?

One day, Joan and I were talking and getting to know each other more. She told me that she and Ken had tried to find out what happened to me, but to no avail; they couldn't get any answers. Joan used to be in the Tuesday morning Bible study I was in. After the accident, the women in this Bible study and Joan prayed for me. They prayed for the girl who was hit by a Mack truck on the side of the highway. These were the same women I was in Bible study with.

Joan asked Pastor Rick's wife if we could share our testimony with the women who had prayed for me in the Bible study. Of course, she agreed. After we shared our experience together with them, it brought tears of joy, an increase of faith, and an answer to all of the prayers they had prayed for me.

I stayed at the Deerfield Church for about a year and a half. During this time, Laura pulled away from her father and me and became pregnant. She rebelled against everything she went through because of me.

Pastor Rick was a great preacher who stuck to God's Word in a very strict manner. He was very honest about sin, marriage, and how you should live your life according to God's Word. I knew abortion was wrong and told Laura to keep the baby and that I would help her raise it. The father of the child was very immature and not ready to be a father. He later left and had nothing to do with the baby.

I will always cherish my time at Deerfield Church, and I'm very grateful for all of Pastor Rick's teachings. But after about a year and a half, I felt a pull from the Holy Spirit to go to The Worship Center. Every time I drove by, I took notice of their sign out front. It said things like, "The joy of the Lord is our strength." I decided to attend one day.

I was getting pretty good at pulling up in a strange parking lot and walking into a church by myself. Of course, God was with me. I walked into The Worship Center. The worship team was playing, and it was just like in Texas. There were people dancing, singing, and praying in tongues. They were worshiping the Lord Jesus with pure abandonment in spirit and in truth. I was finally home!

After the worship was done, a woman named Beth came up to me and welcomed me to the church. She gave me a hug and asked me, "So how long have you been a Christian?"

I said, "About a few years."

She asked, "Have you taken Jesus to be your Lord and Savior?"

I said, "Yes, I was in Texas at my Aunty Noreen's house, and I went to her church and was saved."

She said, "Oh, I know a Noreen Smith in Texas; my parents brought her to the Lord."

I answered, "No way. That's my aunt." God always guides us to the places we need to be at certain times in our lives and gives us divine appointments so we know we're in the right place.

God is amazing. What are the chances I would end up at a church where a woman knew my Aunty Noreen from Texas? Aunty Noreen first brought me to church and led to my salvation. I was standing thousands of miles away, speaking to the woman whose parents brought my Aunty Noreen to the Lord! Praise you, Lord, for you know the beginning from the end!

I made an appointment with Pastor Dean so I could join the worship center. Pastor Dean is an apostle, prophet, teacher, friend, dream interpreter, worship leader, and father of many. He had a pastoral heart. He walks in the Spirit of God twenty-four seven. He has every quality that you would want in a pastor. He has a beautiful wife and family, and they always showed an example you would want to learn from and follow.

I often saw a man named Mike after church when we had coffee, snacks, and fellowship. One day, I had the courage to say hello to him, and we started talking. It's a good thing I did because he was so shy that if I didn't start the conversation, we probably would have never spoken. We eventually started dating and had a lot of fun, both being equally yoked with God.

Mike and I were in a church Easter play together. I invited Joan, Ken, and their family to come to our Easter play. They came to the play, and after it was over, I noticed a necklace on Joan's neck. I asked her where she got it from, and she told me someone from church gave it to her as a present. She said it was her favorite one. This is one of the necklaces I had made and gave to Lydia for her church sale, after my divorce when I lived near the church.

The necklace was given to Joan as a present from the church bazaar. This was before I was saved, while I was still drinking, during the dark part of my life. This necklace was my earth angel, Joan's, favorite necklace! God is an amazing God, right down to every little detail. He brings everything full circle, right down to a necklace I made years ago.

In the Old Testament, in Exodus, Moses and the twelve tribes of Israel traveled and set up the tabernacle for meetings. Everything was done with great precision. Every piece was counted and made for a specific purpose. Each piece of furniture was made from the finest materials, with intricate details, and had a profound significance. There were twelve tribes, and each person in every tribe was accounted for. God is very detail-oriented. At the same time, His love is pure and simple.

The necklace reminds me of how God is so precise when He is trying to get our attention. He sometimes uses common things to make Himself known to us. God shows us all how mighty, powerful, and omnipresent He is, even with such a small detail as a necklace. As I get to know God and have relationship with Him, it never ceases to amaze me. If you keep your eyes on God and wait on Him to show you the heavenly things, you will never be bored. You will only be amazed at His love and beauty that never end. He knows the beginning from the end.

That beautiful man, Mike O'Malley, and I dated. I called him the man with Jesus eyes. He asked me to marry him. At first I said yes, and on Valentine's Day, he took me on a date to a church a few hours away. The worship was awesome, and we were singing to our Valentine, Jesus Christ. I don't remember the sermon, but I knew I was in love!

Mike had three grandsons, and during this time, the middle child became ill with cancer. We spent a lot of time babysitting the three grandsons and, Mike's son, who was about fourteen years old. One of the things I loved about Mike was that he was always a good family man. When his wife left him, he was the one left to bring up his children. We spent a lot of our time at church and with our kids. We went hiking at Waterfall Reservoir on dates alone, and we had some picnics there with our kids. We went to the beach and had a lot of good times.

Then as time went on, there seemed to be some interference with our children. When people are divorced, have children at home and are dating, getting engaged to be married doesn't always go very well. We had some parenting issues, most likely coming from different backgrounds and cultures. There were also some dating issues. I needed more time to heal from some of my past hurts, and I also couldn't understand some of Mike's decisions. After going through two terrible divorces, I decided I was definitely not ready to get married again. So I ran away from Mike and ran away from The Worship Center, but I never ran away from God.

Mike was bewildered and did not completely understand what had just happened. How could I just up and leave? He was very hurt, sad, and confused. I was not well or responsible enough to explain my feelings to him. I couldn't even understand them myself. Mike, being a great man of God, just put it in God's hands, prayed a lot, and never let the thought go that God told him that I was the one he was going to marry.

Mike's life just went on as usual. He stayed very involved in church and with the kids. In the midst of it all, about a year later, his grandson passed away from cancer at three and a half years old. I remember it well. Laura and I attended the wake and funeral. I wanted to be there for Mike as well as his family, as I had always loved him. This was the first time we had seen each other since the breakup.

Mike and I kept in touch over the years. He came to my granddaughter, Shantel's, birthday party, and at different points in life, we connected. Somehow, we always remained friends.

CHAPTER 9

Three Steps Forward, Two Steps Back

Laura had a beautiful baby girl on July 22, 2003. Her name is Shantel Rose, named after my mom. She was a new and precious joy in my life!

Things were going well for me; I landed a great job at the post office and worked my way up to the human resources department. I had some really great friends and a great support system.

I drove an hour to work and back every day. Because of the traveling, I sold my house, and moved with my daughter and granddaughter into a nice four-bedroom house closer to work. It had a beautiful backyard that I decorated with flowers. I kept up the landscaping and had great neighbors, an older couple who loved to hear me practice worshiping from my porch at night. I was settled nicely in my life.

I went to a Catholic church every morning to pray at 7:00 a.m. before work, and that was the extent of my fellowship with brothers and sisters in Christ. But I had to find other support groups to go to and meet all new friends, even though Naomi was still my best friend. Because I played music, I started going to open mics where they had no alcohol and began playing Christian music. I also played good secular music and songs I wrote myself.

Naomi and I went to a few campouts every year where they had different workshops, and I learned much about myself. I've learned how to forgive others for the terrible abuse I suffered, knowing that we are all sinners and fall short of the glory of God. I learned about different family cycles or curses we all carry from our past and that it was time to end the cycle. I learned why abusers abuse and how to forgive them.

There is much freedom in forgiveness. I now can dance with God, sing praises to Him, and enjoy my life. If we listen to what God is trying to show us and let Him into our hearts, we can allow Him to heal us from past traumas and abuses. He took just enough pain out of my past so I could bear the rest and have the strength to honestly look through my life.

We always say God never gives us more than we can handle. I believe this is true with all my heart. Through God's love, mercy, and grace, He put beautiful people in my path. I made the choice to let them in to help me heal, and because of this, I am a better person today.

As time went on, I began to play at the festivals, and I began to draw attention from men that I certainly wasn't ready for. During my healing time from alcoholism, I hadn't put myself in a relationship or let myself fall for a man. Then I started playing music with a man and began to date him. I grew further and further from God and fell into sin. I slept with this man.

I have no idea what on earth I was doing. I fell, slipped, and went two steps backward. But when you're pretty and playing music, people tend to fall in love with the person on the stage, not who you really are. I became a popular person on the stage, and it went straight to my head. I felt beautiful, talented, and loved by many for the first time in my life. Unknowingly, I was being tempted and pulled once again by the darkness. They were drawn to the light inside of me, the gift that God gave me, and instead of me bringing them into relationships with Jesus, I was falling deeper into sin.

74

After three years of loving life and getting blessed by God, my sin took everything away from me that I loved the most. First, my daughter became pregnant with her second child and moved to Arizona with the father. It was the worst day of my life. My Shantel and Laura were gone; my heart was broken into a million pieces. The man I dated and sinned with cheated on me, my beautiful babies were gone. I never ceased to pray for them every day. I prayed for God to take care of them and for their healing and salvation.

Life was good for a few years until winter came around. It was getting harder and harder for me to get out of bed in the morning. I was in excruciating pain. It took me about an hour and a half just to get ready for work. Every day, I got down on my knees and begged God to help me through each day.

Because of the accident, the doctors said that I had fibromyalgia. After going to several doctors, the pain would not stop. I had no idea how I would be able to pay a mortgage. I found myself alone in a four-bedroom house, just existing. I heard that the warm climate in Texas would be better for my physical condition.

When I decided to move to Texas, Mike called me and tried his hardest to talk me out of it. I told him that he didn't understand the pain I was in, and I had no other option. In my heart of hearts, I hoped he would ask me to marry him again, and we could be together forever, but I did not want to burden him with my life at the time. I had absolutely nothing to offer. I sold everything and went to live in Texas with my parents. I guess at this time, God had other plans for both of us.

CHAPTER 10

Homesick

I ended up moving to Texas. It was sunny, bright, and beautiful. My home was a five-minute drive from the lake, and I found an awesome church right down the street. I became involved in the children's ministries there.

The pain seemed to feel better in the warm climate. I would get a coffee at the shop, go the lake, read and drink my coffee in the morning. It was a very good time in my life. Pastor Don was a riot. His sermons were down-to-earth so people could understand them; at the same time, they had a very deep biblical meaning for others going deeper in God's Word.

I started seeing my dad's doctor in Texas. Weather changes, humidity, and especially storms gave me terrible pain. My doctor would give me pain medicine, and I received epidural shots just like in New England. I only took the medications when I absolutely needed them, not as prescribed.

This new doctor suggested that I see a neurological psychiatrist so he could do a neuropsychiatric evaluation to find out what parts of my brain were still working and what parts were not. I found out that my brain was bruised on the left side, which controls equation, memory, and reasoning. The right side is the creative, artistic, and discerning side. I know God saved the right side of my brain so I could still write and play music.

I also found that my brain at this time was functioning at about a seventeen- to twenty-one-year-old level. I was still very childish and grieved my past before the accident when I could ride horses and do physical activities that I was now incapable of doing.

I had a really hard time with grownups, and sometimes I still do because of the way they complicate the simplest things in life. It is because of God's favor, mercy and grace that I receive His help, and I praise God, for He is always there for me. This unconditional love that God has for me helps me find myself in this wonderful place of humility, and I find myself seeking to understand how to give that same love to others.

Going to church and working with the children was my speed at the time. I wanted to be on the worship team that played music in the church in the morning. But God knew right where I belonged—with the children! Teaching the children brought me deep into God's Word, and I learned more about God and what kind of response He was looking for from the ones desperately seeking His face and heart.

God doesn't always give us what we want, but He gives us what we need. God also knows the desires of our hearts, and He loves us so much that He can't wait for the right timing to bless us.

I loved working with the children. I was blessed with great friendships that grew with the children and others involved in the ministry. Most of the people at church dressed very formally, and we were blessed to be able to wear jeans and T-shirts! This was another door God opened for me, as I am more comfortable in casual clothes. I was at church more than I was home, and I could wear jeans!

I went to Wednesday night Bible study, taught Bible lessons with the kids three times a week, and went to one of the services on Sunday. The children I taught in Bible school became very dear to me.

On Tuesday and Saturday nights in coffee shops, I played my guitar and sang some uplifting secular songs mixed in with Christian songs and songs that I wrote. This gave me extra money. I also played music with some friends I had made in another support group who were incredibly talented musicians. I found it quite surprising how most people would respond to the originals and Christian music, especially the young adults who came on a regular basis and sang along, having no idea God's hand was in all of it, planting seeds. Most people would think that this was the perfect life, and it was.

As time went by, I began to feel lonely. I found myself alone on the porch at night, telling God, "There must be more than this, Lord." I would have visits from friends at home, but being from a small town in New England, I was missing home.

I became very homesick. Naomi and her daughter came down for my birthday. That year, my birthday fell on Thanksgiving Day. I love to cook! My parents had some friends over, and I cooked Thanksgiving dinner for about eighteen people. I was very blessed to have my best friend visit! We did a lot that week; I could barely keep up with her. When they left, I missed New England and my friends more than ever.

CHAPTER 11

The Wedding Feast

Mike and I always remained friends, even though we didn't always see each other. God had some divine appointments when we got together. Some were good times, and some were hard times.

Out of the blue, I called him one night. We started chatting at least once a week, which turned into every night. My heart longed for home. One day, we were on the phone, and I told him I was playing in New Hampshire and would be home for another week after that. I asked if we could get together. He told me that there was a leadership conference that week and asked if I was able to attend. He said, "All you have to do is sign up online." I signed up, and after I was done playing in New Hampshire, I went to the conference. Mike and I were able to spend some real quality time together.

I stayed at an Inn in New Hampshire which was a beautifully restored antique home with a baby grand piano in the sitting room. I thought I would treat myself because my camping days were over. With all my aches and pains, I couldn't sleep in a tent out in the elements anymore. I was everyone's weather girl. I knew when it was going to rain, how hard, and approximately how long it would last.

I spent time practicing with my friend, J. R., who came up later. J. R. and I played music together all the time. He knew all my songs, and I knew his. When I played guitar, I just played rhythm, so it was always nice to have an accomplished lead player and friend during the instrumentals.

To my surprise, I woke up on Saturday morning to a knock on my door. I opened the door, and there was Mike! I was in my pajamas, and I asked, "Mike, what are you doing here?" and shut the door in His face. I was not ready for this, standing there in my pajamas. I threw on some clothes on and ran out the door.

I found Mike outside in the parking lot. He had put a note on my door with flowers, and when I went outside, he asked me to marry him. I told him that I was really bad at relationships, and he really didn't want to marry me. He asked me again, "Sarah, will you marry me?" I told him that I would marry him under two conditions. The first one was that I would marry him as long as Pastor Dean married us. The second related to a Scripture that we had for each other a long time ago from the book of Ruth.

> Entreat me not to leave you, Or to turn back from following after you: For wherever you go, I will go; And wherever you lodge, I will lodge; Your people shall be my people, And your God, my God, When you die, I will die, And there will I be buried. The Lord do so to me, and more also, If anything but death parts you and me. (Ruth 1:16–17)

I reminded him of this Scripture and said, "These people are my people. If you can stay the weekend and know that this is a huge part of my life and still want to marry me, then I will marry you." After the weekend, we were engaged.

I went to the leadership conference following the long weekend and spent more time with my new fiancé. We both knew I had to go back to Texas before he could bring me home for our wedding. We went to a jewelry store, and he bought me an engagement ring. I still have it on my finger; it's the most beautiful ring I have ever seen. It's multifaceted, just like the ministries God has given to us and the ones we haven't even started yet.

After the conference, I had time to spend with my family, and I told them all the news. Of course, since this was my third marriage, they were happy for me but said, "Just keep it small."

Mike and I prayed for a date for our wedding and came up with the numbers one and two. We thought it was for the number twelve. As we prayed, we knew that it was going to be in September. The twelfth of September was not available. We prayed some more and came up with September 21. This would be the day of our wedding.

We later learned that September 21 landed on Yom Kippur. This was very important to me because my mom was Jewish. This is the holiest day for Jewish people and a day for atonement, repentance, and a new beginning. After the Jewish people fast and pray for repentance, they have a huge feast and celebration.

Mike came to Texas and helped me move back to New England and bring my things back with me. We loaded up my SUV, and he helped me drive home.

I remember the day of our wedding like it was yesterday. It was a beautiful fall day in September. The weather was perfect, and Pastor Dean married us. Pastor Beth spoke of Yom Kippur, and Mary, the pastor's wife, played the most beautiful music I'd ever heard. We were married right at the time Yom Kippur was beginning. It was the beginning of our new life together.

Right before the end of the ceremony, before Pastor Dean pronounced us man and wife, he blew the Shofar, and we marked the beginning of Yom Kippur, became husband and wife, and had our first kiss at the altar. It was a new beginning to our new life together, and it was beautiful! Mike and I had a big reception with all the bells and whistles. We both looked at it like our first real wedding, under God.

Mike's boss gave us a house to stay at for a week in Martha's Vineyard for our wedding present. It was beautiful there. We spent time at the beach, did a little shopping, and enjoyed quiet dinners at the beach house. After that, we went back to New Hampshire to the beautiful Inn, where he first asked me to marry him. We enjoyed our stay there; this was the beginning of our relationship as a couple. I'm truly blessed to be married to the most kind, loving, and compassionate man, Mike.

CHAPTER 12

Back to My First Love

Mike and I are now married, and we went through many trials and tribulations. We included all our children and grandchildren in our wedding, believing that involving them would bring us all close together. I thought that we would have family Sunday dinners and the family would get together for cookouts and other fun activities.

Mike's youngest child was eighteen, and all our other children lived on their own with their own children. I unknowingly assumed everything would be different. Unfortunately, because of our children's pasts, the divorces, and deep wounds that never healed, this would not be an easy ride.

My daughter went through a lot of changes, and she was happy for us. However, Mike's children never really accepted me as their stepmother. I tried to bring the family closer but to no avail. To this day, I don't know if they thought I was trying to take their mother's place or what kind of scars they have from past hurts, even though I told them I just wanted to be a friend to them. I never wanted to take their mother's place, and I felt at one time we were beginning to have a good relationship. But somewhere along the way, there was a severed relationship with one child. I will never cease to pray for complete healing and restoration for our family relationships.

It takes time and a lot of prayer for children to let other adults into their lives. I just think about how long it took me to look at the cup as half full instead of empty. Time, love, and lots of prayer heal all wounds.

Because of the accident, I was diagnosed with depression, chronic muscle pain, arthritis, and fibromyalgia. I get through the depression by relying on God's power, grace, and love to bring me through each day. I don't believe that anyone in this world could go through all this without the help of our Lord Jesus Christ. This is how I can look at the cup as half full instead of half empty. When I feel depressed, I just get back down on my knees and ask God for His help to get me through each day.

Back in New England, I had a new doctor who put me on narcotic medications and gave me epidural, neck, and shoulder injections of steroids for the pain. It's funny how much we trust doctors and rely solely on what they say. I did not take the narcotic medications as prescribed. I only took them in the winter when I couldn't get out of bed or when my pain was unmanageable. In the spring, after most of the pain subsided, I got off the medicine completely.

Every winter, I began to have pain in my back, neck, and hip and went back to the doctors for spinal injections. I sometimes needed to take medications just to get out of bed. This went on for about five years. In the spring, I got off the medications again.

In the spring of 2009, The Worship Center had a month of healing with prophets, doctors, and teachers speaking each week. I related to the first prophet who came. He had a near-death experience and saw Jesus more than once.

On a Friday night, he had a word from God about people on medications. He said that there were too many Christian addicted to narcotics. If you're addicted to narcotics, you should see a doctor and get off all narcotic medications. Cry out to the Lord, and in twenty-eight days, the Lord will heal you. He said that if you are on narcotic medications, you should see a doctor and try to get off of them.

For me, it was a prophetic word from God. Although I would not suggest this to anyone under any circumstances, that night, I decided to stop all my medications at once. Of course, I had nothing to fear. I wasn't addicted to them—or so I thought.

Because I didn't feel like I was addicted to my medications, I never thought what was about to happen would come to pass. I dumped all of the prescriptions I had out, and I started detoxing at home.

As I lay in my bed, I had night sweats, my heart raced, and I was afraid that I was going to die. I threw up day after day, shaking and crying out to the Lord, singing out worship songs while my breath became faint. The first few days were the worst. I didn't think I was going to make it through the days or nights. I drew all the shades and was paranoid and afraid someone would actually see me in this condition.

I have a beautiful husband who cares for me. I was a forty-six-year-old woman weighing about ninety pounds soaking wet, begging God to help me get through this. I tried to go to every church healing service I could for that month, desperately seeking to hear God's Word, as my condition kept getting worse and worse. I couldn't make them all.

There were three more prophets, healers, and speakers. One speaker's wife had her doctorate in science and put it to good use with biblical knowledge. She taught us how to deliver ourselves (get rid of past hurts) while doing a thing called dropping down. So I started dropping down quite a few times a day, sometimes for an hour, sometimes longer. It seemed that I got rid of some more baggage from my past and was healing my inner man (my spirit).

The only problem, as these weeks went by, I became colder. The touch of my hand was almost like ice. It was near the last weekend—about the twenty-seventh day—when a couple who had done much deliverance prayer and ministry for me in my earlier walk with Christ came walking in the door. I said, "Hi" and touched her neck.

She said, "Oh, your hands are so cold". My heart beat became slower and slower. I kept crying out to the Lord nonetheless. I believed and had faith in the word the first prophet had said, about crying out for the Lord's healing for twenty-eight days. If you believe and have a very strong faith in God, I believe He can heal you from anything.

> Bless the Lord, O my soul; And all that is within me, bless His holy name! Bless the Lord, O my soul, And forget not all His benefits; Who forgives all your iniquities, Who heals all your diseases, Who redeems your life from destruction, Who crowns you with lovingkindness and tender mercies, Who satisfies your mouth with good things, So that your youth is renewed like the eagle's. (Psalm 103:1–5)

It was the last night of the healing month at The Worship Center. I walked in the door and saw Pastor Dean. I said, "Hi, Pastor Dean; it's been twenty-eight days." He said, "Hi" and looked at me funny. I don't believe he knew what I was talking about.

The end of the service was at about 10:00 p.m. Mike's birthday was the next day. I felt like my heart was going to stop beating. My face was pale, and my skin was clammy. I thought I was going to die that night to be forever with my beloved Jesus. As we put our coats on, I slowly put my pocketbook on my shoulder. I said, "God, it's the twenty-eighth day, and you promised."

I turned around in that moment and saw Eric, the worship leader and a good friend, coming toward me. He asked, "Can I pray on you?" He had a very serious look on his face, like he was on a mission from God—and he was. He started to pray by putting his hand on my head, and I started to shake in the Spirit. After a few minutes, he asked Mike to put his hand over my heart and asked me to put mine over Mike's. Then Eric put both his hands over ours and started praying.

My body leaned backward and shook as he prayed. I knew that God was healing me and holding me up. As he prayed, he said, "God is now giving you a Holy Ghost blood transfusion, and the blood of Jesus is running back and forth through your veins." I could feel the flow of the Holy Spirit and the new blood running through my veins.

This went on for a while. Then Eric said, "You're totally and completely healed in the name of Jesus Christ. I'm not the one telling you this; God is telling you that you are completely healed—completely."

I fell down in the power of Holy Spirit. I don't know how long I lay there, but when I stood up, I felt like a new woman. I said to Mike, who was standing over me, "Happy birthday, honey. You have your wife back."

As we left, I went over and thanked Eric for being obedient to God. He said, "It's been nice knowing you."

> Then your light shall break forth like the morning,
> Your healing shall spring forth speedily, And your
> righteousness shall go before you; The glory of the
> Lord shall be your rear guard. Then you shall call,
> and the Lord will answer; You shall cry, and He
> will say, "Here I am." (Isaiah 58:8–11)

God is rich in mercy and grace. He is shaping, restoring, and still refining me into the woman of God he has created me to be. At times, I still fall short of the glory of God. But I bow on my knees in repentance. I wake up every morning and read His Word and worship Him. Through prayer and meditation, I ask Him to help me through the day.

My mind is much clearer now, and I will not let anything come between me and God. He is the lover of my soul, my strength, my peace, and the love that guides me. I believe that he sends His angels down to tend to His children when they are in need.

It's been over seven years now since Mike and I have been married. I am very active in church, I am completely healed, I have been on a mission trip to Ireland, I am on the Worship team, and I go to prayer every Wednesday night with Mike. God has placed strong women of God in my life that I spend time with, and our church family is great! I'm going on mission trips, and doing outreach in the city. Life couldn't be better. I am still praying for family members to have intimate relations with Jesus.

My hope for you is that it doesn't take a tragedy like getting hit by a Mack truck to bring you into the presence of a loving God. My prayer for you is that you come to take Jesus Christ into your heart and follow the God who created us and everything up to the heavens. You can get to know Him by His word, and take Him into your heart through repentance. I pray that you be given supernatural revelation of the love of Jesus Christ that will bring you into an intimate relationship with Him. That you will come to understand the knowledge of the depths of the love of Jesus Christ has for you. It doesn't matter where you've been what you've done, how far you have gone, it's never too late, God loves you and He is waiting patiently for you to call out His name.

I would like to leave you with one of my favorite Scriptures: "May the Lord bless you and keep you; The Lord make His face shine upon you, And be gracious to you; The Lord lift up His countenance upon you, And give you peace" (Numbers 6:24–26).

CPSIA information can be obtained
at www.ICGtesting.com
Printed in the USA
BVHW030208140421
604886BV00007B/126

9 781490 859231